PURSUING INTIMACY WITH GOD I

www.intimacywithgod.com

God's Greatest Desire

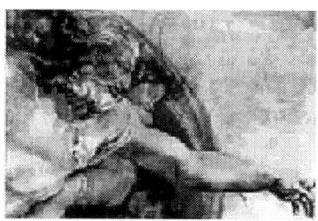 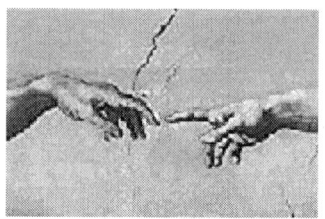

What is God's greatest desire for you ? God sees you as a precious treasure, and He longs to have close fellowship with you. More than anything He wants you to have an intimate love relationship and friendship with Him. God longs for you to spend time with Him daily and intimately communicate with Him, to hear His voice, to enjoy fellowship with Him, to trust and follow Him, and to give your life meaning and purpose.

Do you desire a deeper and closer relationship and friendship with God ? Is your desire to know Him and to please Him growing ? Do you want to know God in real & personal ways, rather than just knowing about Him ? Do you know that hearing God's voice is by far the most important part of your prayer/fellowship time with God ? Because you are precious to Him and He greatly loves you, God wants to be your first love and have first place in your life. If you answered yes to any of these questions, then this in-depth Bible study is for you. Although it may mean making changes in your life and in your daily schedule, you can have the fullest and closest possible fellowship and partnership with God throughout the rest of your life. Any Christian can have this wonderful intimacy with God, and experience the abundant and full and meaningful life that God designed you to have. Always remember that God wants intimacy with you and He wants you to have the abundant life He promises more than you want it. As you seek Him and desire with all of your heart to have an intimate fellowship with God, He will always be there to help you every step of the way.

This 6 week study carefully examines and explores what God designed prayer to be; why you need to pray and spend time with God regularly; how to intimately communicate with God; why it is important to start your day and your prayer & fellowship time with God with praise and worship; how to hear God's voice through His Word and His Spirit speaking to you; how to meditate on God's Word and make sure you correctly observe & hear all you can, so that you can then correctly interpret it and then apply it in your life; why it is vitally important to regularly maintain your intimate fellowship with God by confessing your sins and reconnecting to God; and what God's ultimate goals and plans and calling is for your life. It is our prayer that, through the power and grace of the Holy Spirit, God will greatly bless you in your fellowship and walk with Him through this study, and that He will reveal His glory and beauty to you, and that He will also reveal the wonderful and amazing plans that He has for you. God bless you as you seek intimacy with Him.

"I keep asking that the God of our Lord Jesus Christ, the glorious Father, maygive you the Spirit of wisdom and revelation, so that you may know him better." (Ephesians 1:17)

PURSUING INTIMACY WITH GOD

Welcome to the Pursuing Intimacy With God Bible study. This Bible study and ministry is dedicated to helping you to pursue and ultimately receive the fullest and most intimate fellowship and oneness and partnership with Jesus Christ.

There is one very critical issue that needs to be settled before you can ever begin to deepen your relationship and fellowship with God ... do you have a reconciled personal relationship with God ? What are the requirements and details of Salvation & Gospel of Jesus Christ

There are many people these days that believe that God does not exist. There are many others that believe that God is some far away, impersonal spirit that takes pleasure in punishing people and making their life difficult. Sometimes if a person has had a bad experience with their own father, or had a father that abandoned them, they will have a hard time seeing God for who He really is. And it will then be difficult to personally know God.

The Bible tells us that God is not some far away impersonal spirit. God can seem that way to some people, and it is more challenging to many because God is not visible to us. Acts 17:27 says "that they would seek God, if perhaps they might grope for Him and find Him, though He is not far from each one of us." The Bible promises us in many verses that if we will seek to personally know God, then we will find Him and ultimately know Him.

God is a loving and caring personal love-relationship oriented father. He loves us and He very much desires to have a restored relationship with us. "God desires all men to be saved and to come to the knowledge of the truth." - I Timothy 2:4. God wants everyone to be saved... to first have a restored relationship with Him, then close fellowship with Him, and ultimately eternal life with Him in heaven when our life here is done.

The first important thing in order to begin to know God for who He really is, and have close fellowship with Him and personally know God: You have to have a restored or reconciled relationship with God. God's Word the Bible clearly shows that we all have a broken relationship with God because of our sins, and that we need to have this taken care of. Many people try to solve this problem of sin and separation from God and a broken relationship with Him themselves. People try many things to try to reach out to God and personally know Him... they try Religion, or Philosophy, or Church, or doing good things, or giving money to charity...

Also, we are all created with a built in need to personally know God and have a restored relationship and fellowship with Him. When this need is not met, then we will have a void in our life. Many people do not know what it is, but they will know that something is missing in their life or that something is not right. People will try all types of things to try to fill this void in their life... Relationships with people, Sex, Drugs, Alcohol, Pleasure, Recreation, Money, Career,...

Salvation & The Gospel of Jesus Christ (A Restored Relationship With God):

Step 1 God loves you and wants you to experience peace and life – abundant and eternal life:
- "We have peace with God through our Lord Jesus Christ." – Romans 5:1
- "For God so loved the world that he gave his one and only Son, that whoever believes in

- him shall not perish but have everlasting life." – John 3:16
- God loves you so much that He sent His only Son Jesus to suffer and then die a very painful death on a cross, to make it possible for us to have a restored relationship with Him.
- "I have come that they may have life, and that they may have it more abundantly." – John 10:10

Step 2: The Problem – Our Sin & Separation From God:
- "For all have sinned and fall short of the glory of God." – Romans 3:23
- "For the wages of sin is death (eternal separation from God), but the gift of God is eternal life in Christ Jesus our Lord." – Romans 6:23
- "But your iniquities have separated you from your God; your sins have hidden his face from you, so that he will not hear." – Isaiah 59:2
- Our sins are personally against God, and cause us to have a broken relationship with Him, and to be separated from Him.
- Sin is not just breaking some religious rule or law. Sin is personally against God... "Against You, You only, I have sinned And done what is evil in Your sight, So that You are justified when You speak And blameless when You judge." - Psalm 51:4Our Attempts To Reach God:
- people have tried in many ways to bridge this gap and separation between themselves and God ... good works, religion, philosophy, morality,... and none work ... except One
- "There is a way that seems right to a man, but in the end it leads to death." – Proverbs 14:12
- Jesus said "I am the way, the truth, and the life. No one may come to the Father except through me." – John 14:6

Step 3: God's Solution To Our Problem – Salvation & Gospel of Jesus Christ And The Cross:
- "For there is one God and one mediator between God and men, the man Jesus Christ." – I Timothy 2:5
- "For Christ died for sins once for all, the righteous for the unrighteous, to bring you to God." – I Peter 3:18
- "But God demonstrates his own love for us in this: While we were still sinners, Christ died for us." – Romans 5:8
- Jesus is God's answer and solution to our problem of sin, eternal separation from God, and eternal punishment for our sins.
- "For God so loved the world that he gave his one and only Son, that whoever believes in him shall not perish but have everlasting life." – John 3:16
- Jesus said "I am the way, the truth, and the life. No one may come to the Father *except through me*." – John 14:6

Step 4: Our Response: Repent, Put Your Faith in Jesus, and Receive Christ As Your Lord & Savior:
- you must trust Jesus Christ as your Lord and Savior and receive Him by faith and

personal invitation:
- "Here I am! I stand at the door and knock. If anyone hears my voice and opens the door, I will come in and eat with him, and he with me." – Revelation 3:20
- "That if you confess with your mouth "Jesus is Lord", and believe in your heart that God raised him from the dead, you will be saved." – Romans 10:9
- "Jesus went into Galilee, proclaiming the good news of God. "The time has come," he said. "The kingdom of God has come near. *Repent* and *believe the good news*!" – Mark 1:14-15
- "Yet to all who did *receive him* (Jesus), to those who *believed* in his name (Jesus), he gave the right to become children of God." – John 1:12

Receive Jesus means that you need to commit your life to Him and follow Him as your Lord & Savior. Nearly everyone wants Jesus to be their friend. Nearly everyone also wants Jesus to be their Savior and save them from their sins and the eternal punishment of hell. But many people do not really want Jesus to be their Lord. The Lord of their life. Which means to give up control and the rights to their life to Jesus. It may mean you need to give up your dreams and goals and plans, and accept Jesus' will and plans instead. It may cost you a lot. Their is a cost to follow Jesus as Lord & Savior and be His disciple (a disciple is a learner & follower of Jesus). You need to commit your life to Jesus, and commit to follow Him as your *Lord* and Savior.

If you have never trusted and received Jesus Christ as your Lord and Savior, but you are ready to do so, then you can do it right now. In order to have a restored relationship with God you need to do the 2 things that Jesus said in Mark 1:14-15, and also to receive Jesus as Lord & Savior as in John 1:12 and commit to follow Him:

1. Admit your need ("I am a sinner and I need a savior")
2. Be willing to turn from your sins (repent - Mark 1:14-15).
3. Believe with all of your heart that Jesus loves you and died for your sins and paid the price for them. Believe also that Jesus rose again from the grave after 3 days, and later ascended back to heaven. (Mark 1:14-15 and John 1:12)
4. 4. Through prayer, talk to and invite Jesus Christ to come into your life and be your Lord and Savior, and commit to follow Him in your life:

"Dear Lord, Thank you for loving me very much, and for sending Jesus to die for my sins. Lord, I have sins in my life. Please forgive me for all of my sins. And dear Lord Jesus, please come into my life, and be my Lord and Savior. I commit my life to you, to follow You and Your ways. And I repent and turn away from my sins, and I turn back to you. Please give me peace with God and eternal life in heaven. Please teach me your ways, and help me grow closer to you. In Jesus name. Amen."

If you have done these things – you truly repented of your sins, put all of your faith and hope in Jesus Christ, and received Him as your Lord & Savior and committed your life to follow Him, and you meant it sincerely with all your heart – then now you for sure have a reconciled relationship with God, peace with God and eternal life, and new life in Jesus.

- "Everyone who calls on the name of the Lord will be saved." – Romans 10:13
- "Those who have the Son (Jesus) have life. Those who do not have the Son do not have life. These things have I written, that you may know you have eternal life." – I John 5:12-13

If you have prayed and repented and put your faith in Jesus, and received Him as your Lord & Savior and committed your life to Him, and meant it with all of your heart - Welcome to God's family !!!

Once you have a restored personal relationship with God through Jesus Christ, you can begin to seek to have intimate fellowship with Him and you can get to know God more and more. In Part 2 of this series we will look at what it takes for you to have intimacy with God and how you can know God personally.

PURSUING INTIMACY WITH GOD I

Week 1 - WHAT IS PRAYER ?	P.10-13
- CAN YOU KNOW GOD INTIMATELY ?	14-16
- ARE YOU SEEKING GOD ?	17-18
- Week 1 Study Review (p.19)	
Week 2 - WHY SHOULD YOU SPEND TIME WITH GOD ?	21-26
- YOUR IDENTITY IN CHRIST	27-28
- Week 2 Study Review (p.29-30)	
Week 3 - HOW TO PURSUE INTIMACY WITH GOD	31-32
- VITALS FOR A CLOSE RELATIONSHIP	33-34
- PRAISE & WORSHIP THE LORD	35-37
- PRAISE AS A SPIRITUAL WEAPON	38
- TRUE WORSHIP OF GOD	39-40
- PRAISING GOD FOR WHO HE IS	41-42
- Week 3 Study Review (p.43-44)	
Week 4 - HEAR GOD'S VOICE / READ GOD'S WORD	45-49
- MEDITATE ON GOD'S WORD	50
- ARE YOU SUCCESSFUL ? / WHAT IS SUCCESS ?	51-52
- Week 4 Study Review (p.53-54)	
Week 5 - CONFESS YOUR SINS/ RECONNECT WITH GOD	56-57
- RELATIONSHIP HINDRANCES	58
- IS JESUS YOUR FIRST LOVE ? (IDOLS)	59-62
- PURE PASSION & LOVE FOR JESUS	63
- Week 5 Study Review (p.64-65)	
Week 6 - IT'S THE RELATIONSHIP !!!	66
- GOD'S ULTIMATE GOAL FOR YOU	67-68
- GOD'S CALL	69-72
- SPIRITUAL GIFTS	73-75
- Week 6 Study Review (p.76-77)	

WHAT IS PRAYER ?

Why do you think many Christians do not pray and spend quality time with God daily, like Jesus did ? Some are too busy, some have wrong priorities, some are living for self and not for God, for some the cares of the world have crowded in and robbed them of the joy of having intimate fellowship with God, some have a lack of discipline, some lack faith, some are living in disobedience, some don't know how to pray and have fellowship with God, and some have a wrong understanding of who God is. Many do not understand that God is love relationship oriented, and that His heart's desire is to have close and intimate fellowship with His children. Many do not understand that being a Christian is all about having a growing love relationship with the One who loves them completely and unconditionally, and that it is not about being religious.

* PRAYER IS **VITAL** TO HAVING **INTIMATE FELLOWSHIP** WITH GOD!!!
(God's main call for your life: **I COR. 1:9 "koinania fellowship"**)

("koinania" fellowship- "the fullest possible **fellowship** & **partnership** with God, and with others in the church. Intimate fellowship with God and His son Jesus produces this type of fellowship and unity in a church. Only God can produce this genuine koinania fellowship, love, and unity.")

> always remember that the greatest desire in God's heart is for you to have a growing and intimate love relationship and daily fellowship with Him.

What is the first thing that you think of when you hear the word "prayer" ? Do you think of asking for things ? Praying for someone else ? Or something else ? Let's see what God's Word tells us about what God intends prayer to be:
- PRAYER IS THE **INTIMATE COMMUNICATION** BETWEEN THE HEAVENLY FATHER AND HIS CHILDREN.

"TRUST IN HIM AT ALL TIMES, O PEOPLE; POUR OUT YOUR HEART TO HIM, FOR GOD IS OUR REFUGE" - **PSALM 62:8**

God wants your communication with Him to be honest, open, and transparent. He wants to hear about whatever is in your heart - if you're struggling, or angry, or worried, or anxious, or afraid or hurt,... He cares deeply and wants you to share everything with Him.

* COMMUNICATION IS THE ACT OF MAKING ONE'S SELF UNDERSTOOD; THE EXPRESSION OF ONE'S THOUGHTS & IDEAS & OPINIONS & OF SELF. A GOOD RELATIONSHIP REQUIRES INTIMATE COMMUNICATION.

What is the first thing you think of when you hear the words "eternal life" ? Do you think in terms of time & eternity ? Do you think of heaven ? Or something else ? God defines eternal life as having an intimate relationship & fellowship with Him, where you are getting to know Him more and more, and thus trusting & obeying & following Him. Intimate communication with God is vital to getting to know God better, and hearing His voice is critical to knowing Him and His plans and agenda and dreams for you and your life.

"NOW THIS IS **ETERNAL LIFE:** THAT THEY MAY **KNOW YOU,** THE ONLY TRUE GOD, AND JESUS CHRIST, WHOM YOU HAVE SENT." - JOHN 17:3

"… THAT YOU MAY **KNOW** AND BELIEVE ME, AND UNDERSTAND THAT I AM HE." - ISAIAH 43:10

- also see EXODUS 33:11, 13-18 and PSALM 142:1-6

See "To Know God" (pages 14-15) - the Biblical words for "know God" mean much more than our English word, which sounds like it means to know **about** God. God wants you to **know** Him by seeing and experiencing Him in and around your life. When you see and experience God's faithfulness in your life for example, you then know that God is faithful. This is a much better and more intimate and real knowledge of God than just knowing about Him.

* GOOD COMMUNICATION REQUIRES 2 PEOPLE (GOD COMMUNICATES WITH US AND WE COMMUNICATE WITH HIM IN PRAYER)

A close and intimate relationship needs to be a 2-way relationship. Intimate communication needs to be 2-way also, or it is not good communication. Hearing God's voice is by far the **most important** part of our prayer and fellowship time with Him. If you are not hearing God's voice, you are missing out on getting to know Him more, you will miss His plans for you, and you will miss out on the full & abundant life that He wants you to have, which is only found in Him.

* INTIMACY WITH GOD COMES AS YOU **DESIRE** & **SEEK** TO KNOW HIM, HIS WILL & PLANS, AND HIS WAYS
- Review "ARE YOU SEEKING GOD ?" (Pages 16-17)
- The Greek words for Pray or Prayer mean: to **want**, to **desire**, to **long for**, to ask or beg; great poverty or lack or need; a seeking or asking of God ; to pray earnestly or fervently
- The Hebrew & Greek words for Seek mean: to seek the face of God, to **desire**, to examine or explore, to seek earnestly, to diligently search for, to **crave**, to investigate, to **pursue**
- "I will give them a heart to know me ." — **Jeremiah 24:7**

God needs to touch all of our hearts so that He is our first love and we will seek to know Him

* PRAYER/TIME WITH GOD IS VITAL TO BEING CLOSER TO GOD, "ONE" WITH GOD, AND TO GROWING MORE LIKE JESUS (SPIRITUAL GROWTH)
    read John 17: 20-21 , Exodus 34:28-35 , and Romans 8:28-29

"Prayer is designed more to adjust you to God, than to adjust God to you & your desires."
- Oswald Chambers

"The time a Christian gives to prayer & fellowship with God is not meant for his/her carnal or natural life, but to **nourish** the life of Jesus in him/her." — Oswald Chambers

* **PRAYER IS A GREAT PRIVILEGE** FOR A SINNER TO COME INTO THE PRESENCE OF THE ALMIGHTY & HOLY GOD, AND COMMUNICATE & FELLOWSHIP WITH HIM.

* PRAYER IS A MINISTRY THAT WE ALL ARE TO PARTICIPATE IN; PRAYER IS **DOING GOD'S WORK**.

"If you have so much business to attend to that you have no time to pray, depend upon it, you have more business on hand than God ever intended you should have." - D.L. Moody

God's Word shows that our prayers touch God's heart, and He will respond and work in others' lives when we call upon Him and intercede for others.

* PRAYER IS GOD'S WAY FOR HIS CHILDREN TO ASK HIM FOR THE THINGS THEY NEED & DESIRE, AND TO **SEE & EXPERIENCE** HIS GOODNESS, MERCY, GRACE, FAITHFULNESS,....

- "Taste and see that God is good." — **Psalm 34:8**

* **CLOSE FELLOWSHIP WITH GOD** AND PRAYER IS THE KEY TO UNLOCKING **GOD'S POWER**: (POWER FOR YOUR LIFE, AND POWER FOR CHANGING THE PEOPLE & THE WORLD AROUND YOU)

It is not the act of prayer itself that is the key to unlocking God's power. Many people and churches perform the act of prayer, but yet they are dead. When you have a close and right fellowship with God you will then have a powerful prayer life. Focus and concentrate on your fellowship with God first.

- "The prayer of a **righteous** man is powerful and effective." - James 5:16b

"Anyone who takes the time to enter into an intimate love relationship with God can see God do extraordinary things through his or her life." - Experiencing God

"The closer you get to God, the greater the impact you will have on others' lives. - Top Gun Training

"To be little with God is to be little for God." - E.M. Bounds

* SPENDING TIME WITH GOD/PRAYER IS WHERE THE SPIRITUAL BATTLES ARE FOUGHT AND WON ; GOD'S VICTORIES AND BLESSINGS ARE WON IN YOUR PRAYER TIME WITH GOD:

- read Ephesians 6:10-18

- 2 Corinthians 2:14 - "But thanks be to God, who always leads us as captives in Christ's triumphal procession and uses us to spread the aroma of the knowledge of him everywhere."

- Proverbs 21:30-31 - "There is no wisdom, no insight, no plan that can succeed against the Lord. The horse is made ready for the day of battle, but victory rests with the Lord."

- Psalm 33:10-11 - "The LORD foils the plans of the nations; he thwarts the purposes of the peoples. 11But the plans of the LORD stand firm forever, the purposes of his heart through all generations."

"LORD, the God of our ancestors, are you not the God who is in heaven? You rule over all the kingdoms of the nations. Power and might are in your hand, and no one can withstand you... Our God, will you not judge them? For we have no power to face this vast army that is attacking us. We do not know what to do, but our eyes are on you." — 2 Chronicles 20:6, 12

"This is what the Lord says to you: 'Do not be afraid or discouraged because of this vast army. For the battle is not yours, but God's." — 2 Chronicles 20:15-16

"The one concern of the devil is to keep the saints from prayer. He fears nothing from prayerless studies, prayerless work, prayerless religion. He laughs at our toil, he mocks at our wisdom, but he trembles when we pray."
— Jonathan Edwards

PRAYER IS POWER !

CAN YOU KNOW GOD INTIMATELY ?

There are many people these days that believe that God does not exist. There are many others that believe that God is some far away, impersonal spirit that takes pleasure in punishing people and making their life difficult. Sometimes if a person has had a bad experience with their own father, or had a father that abandoned them, they will have a hard time seeing God for who He really is. And it will then be difficult to personally know God.

The Bible tells us that God is not some far away impersonal spirit. God can seem that way to some people, and it is more challenging to many because God is not visible to us. **Acts 17:27** says "that they would seek God, if perhaps they might grope for Him and find Him, though He is not far from each one of us." The Bible promises us in many verses that if we will seek to personally know God, then we will find Him and ultimately know Him.

God is a loving and caring personal love-relationship oriented father. He loves us and He very much desires to have a restored relationship with us. "God desires all men to be saved and to come to the knowledge of the truth." - **I Timothy 2:4**. God wants everyone to be saved... to first have a restored relationship with Him, then close fellowship with Him, and ultimately eternal life with Him in heaven when our life here is done.

The first important thing in order to begin to know God for who He really is, and have close fellowship with Him and personally know God: You have to have a restored or reconciled relationship with God. God's Word the Bible clearly shows that we all have a broken relationship with God because of our sins, and that we need to have this taken care of. Many people try to solve this problem of sin and separation from God and a broken relationship with Him themselves. People try many things to try to reach out to God and personally know Him... they try Religion, or Philosophy, or Church, or doing good things, or giving money to charity...

Also, we are all created with a built in need to personally know God and have a restored relationship and fellowship with Him. When this need is not met, then we will have a void in our life. Many people do not know what it is, but they will know that something is missing in their life or that something is not right. People will try all types of things to try to fill this void in their life... Relationships with people, Sex, Drugs, Alcohol, Pleasure, Recreation, Money, Career,...

Can you know God personally & intimately, and be His friend ? What does it take to know God personally ?

To know God means much more than just knowing about God. God wants us to know Him and His love & mercy & goodness,... in very personal and real ways. He wants us to enjoy His presence in our lives, and to see and join Him in His activity & work around us.

- "This is Eternal Life: that they may *know you*, the only true God, and Jesus Christ, whom You have sent." – John 17:3

- ".... So that you may *know and believe* Me (God), and understand that I am He." – Isaiah 43:10

- "Teach me your ways so that I may *know you* and continue in your favor." - Exodus 33:13

OLD TESTAMENT

Can you know God personally ? The Bible indicates that you can. The Hebrew word "yada" is used in the Old Testament and is translated in English as the word "Know" or "Knowledge".

The Hebrew word yada has a much wider sweep and meaning than the English word know. The Biblical Old Testament word for Know God personally means the following; to know God means:

- to Perceive
- to Learn
- to Understand
- to Recognize
- to Believe
- to Accept His Claims
- to Conform
- to Be Willing
- to Perform or Live (to please God)
- to Obey
- to See or Experience

Can you know God personally ? The above English words that come out of the Hebrew word "yada" all hold important keys to getting to know God personally, the way that He wants us to know Him. Not just to know about God, but to know Him personally and in real ways by experiencing & seeing Him in your life.

The opposite of knowing God is not ignorance or a lack of knowledge, but is Rebellion. The things that hinder our knowing God personally are a lack of faith, a lack of conforming or submitting to Him, disobedience, and rebellion.

NEW TESTAMENT

The Greek words "oida" and "ginosko" are used in the New Testament for Knowing God. They have the wider meanings as the Hebrew word "yada", but in the context that they are used in the New Testament, they also have the following additional meaning: to know God means:

- to Believe & Receive Jesus (John 1:12)
- to Know Truth (John 14:6)
- to Know Jesus is to Know God (Hebrews 1:1-3)
- to Respond in Faith (Mark 1:14-15, John 1:12)

Can you know God personally and intimately? In order to truly know God personally, first you have to repent (turn away from) of your sins. Then you need to place all of your faith in His Son Jesus Christ (not in a religion, or a church, or in good works... only in Jesus), and also commit your life to follow Jesus and receive Him as your Lord and Savior.

Once you have a restored relationship with God through faith in Jesus, you begin a new relationship and fellowship with Him. It is a long process to grow closer to God, to grow in your faith in Him, and to be transformed to Jesus' image and character (see Romans 8:28-29) and His will, and to become like Him. It requires spending a lot of time with God and seeking Him.

It is possible to know God in personal and real ways. Your heart has to be right towards God. You need to seek Him and spend time with Him, in order for you to know God personally. In His word the Bible God promises that if we seek Him we will find Him (and ultimately you can know God personally).

- "O, the fullness, the pleasure, the sheer excitement of knowing God on earth."
  – Jim Elliott

- "Teach me Your ways, so that I may know you, and continue to find favor with You."
  – Moses (Exodus 33:13)

- "I consider everything a loss compared to the surpassing greatness of knowing Christ Jesus my Lord, for whose sake I have lost all things." – Paul (Philippians 3:7-10)

ARE YOU SEEKING GOD ?

* The Old Testament and New Testament words for "seek" mean: to seek the face of God; to **desire** ; to examine or explore ; to seek earnestly ; to diligently search for ; to wish for; to **crave** ; to investigate ; to pursue.

* Only God can touch our hearts and give us the desire to seek and to know Him, and to want His will & plans & ways above our own:

" I will give them a heart to **know me**." – **Jeremiah 24:7**

" O Lord, God of our fathers, keep this desire in the hearts of your people forever, and keep their hearts loyal to you. And give my son Solomon the wholehearted devotion to keep your commands, requirements, and decrees…" – **I Chronicles 29:18-19**

"For it is God who works in you to will and act according to His good purpose." – **Phil. 2:13**

* Intimacy with God and the fullest possible **fellowship** and **partnership** with Him comes as you **desire** and **seek** to know Him, His plans, will and His ways. Prayer and spending time with God is all about **desire & passion for God** ; it is not a "religious" discipline in your Christian walk.

"If you are pleased with me, teach me your ways, so I may know you and continue to find favor with you… Show me your glory." – Moses (**Exodus 33:13,18**)

" One thing I ask of the Lord, this is what I seek; that I may dwell in the house (presence) of the Lord all the days of my life, to gaze upon the beauty of the Lord and to seek Him in his temple." (**Psalm 27:4**)

"As the deer pants for streams of water, so my soul pants for you, O God. My soul thirsts for God, for the living God. When can I go and meet with God ? – Sons of Korah (**Psalm 42:1-2**)

" O God, you are my God, earnestly I seek you; my soul thirsts for you, my body longs for you, in a dry and weary land where there is no water. I have seen you in the sanctuary and beheld your power and your glory… you love is better than life…" – David (**Psalm 63:1-3**)

" How lovely is your dwelling place, O Lord Almighty ! My soul yearns even faints for the courts of the Lord; my heart and my flesh cry out for the living God." – David (**Psalm 84:1-2**)

" Now devote your heart and souls to seeking the Lord your God." – **I Chronicles 22:19**

" And you my son Solomon, acknowledge the God of your father, and serve him with wholehearted devotion and with a willing mind, for the Lord searches every heart and understands every motive behind the thoughts. If you seek Him he will be found by you; but if you forsake Him, He will reject you forever." – **I Chronicles 28:9**

" For I know the plans I have for you, plans to prosper you and not to harm you, plans to give you hope and a future. Then you will call upon me and come and pray to me, and I will listen to you. You will seek me and find me when you seek me with all your heart.
– **Jeremiah 29:11-13**

" I consider everything a loss compared to the surpassing greatness of knowing Christ Jesus my Lord, for whose sake I have lost all things. I consider them rubbish that I may gain Christ... I want to know Christ and the power of his resurrection..."
– Paul (**Philippians 3:7-11**)

Other verses to read:
- Hosea 10:12
- James 4:8
- Deuteronomy 4:29
- 2 Chronicles 15:2

"Whoever **pursues** righteousness and love finds life, prosperity and honor." - Proverbs 21:21

"But **seek first** his kingdom and his righteousness, and all these things will be given to you as well. - Matthew 6:33

WEEK 1 STUDY REVIEW (Pages 10-18)

q PRAYER IS MUCH, MUCH MORE THAN JUST ASKING GOD FOR THINGS. MARK THE STATEMENTS THAT ACCURATELY DESCRIBE PRAYER:
___ Prayer is absolutely vital to having an intimate relationship with God.
___ Prayer is intimate communication between God and you.
___ True, intimate communication is open and honest.
___ The most important part of prayer is listening to God.
___ Prayer is about seeking to get all that you want from God.
___ Prayer is about seeking to know God, and seeking to know His will and His ways, and seeking His presence and activity in your life and all around you.
___ Prayer is designed to adjust God to you and your desires.
___ Prayer is a ministry that is only for people who are gifted in this area.
___ Prayer is where spiritual warfare is fought and won.

q ETERNAL LIFE IS BEST DESCRIBED IN THE BIBLE AS (JOHN 17:3,...) :
___ Asking Jesus to save you from your sins, and then waiting until you go to heaven.
___ Having a restored relationship with God by fully trusting in Jesus and what He did at the cross, getting to know God in real & personal ways by humbly seeking and then obeying & following Him, and serving Him and others because you love Him.

q CHECK THE ITEMS THAT THE OLD TESTAMENT WORD FOR KNOWING GOD MEANS (See "To Know God" - Page 14-16):
___ To perceive and understand ___ To gain intellectual knowledge
___ To believe ___ To accept His claims
___ To be willing and obey ___ To know about Him
___ To be in control of your own life ___ To go to church
___ To see or experience ___ To be a deacon

q WHICH STATEMENTS BEST DESCRIBE WHAT IT MEANS TO KNOW GOD:
___ God wants you to attain knowledge from the Bible and know more about Him.
___ God wants you to know Him in real and personal ways.
___ God wants you to see and know that He is loving, faithful, good, patient, forgiving...

q CHECK THE ITEMS THAT BEST DESCRIBE THE MEANING OF "SEEK" GOD:
___ To pray and ask and seek God to bless you and your own plans and desires
___ To have a strong desire in your heart for God, and to know Him & His will and plans
___ To pursue your own dreams and goals
___ To pursue God, and to want His plans and agenda above your own
___ To examine and explore (see Acts 17:11-12)
___ To wish for or to crave - for God, not just for His blessing and gifts.

q WHICH STATEMENT DO YOU THINK IS MOST ACCURATE ?
___ Prayer is the key to unlocking God's power in my life and in my ministry for Him.
___ A close and right relationship with God and Prayer is the key to unlocking God's power in my life and in my ministry for Him.

Get face to face with God and prayerfully review this week's material. Ask God to show you how you can be closer to Him and more one with Him

WHY SHOULD YOU PRAY & SPEND TIME WITH GOD ?

God sees you as a precious treasure, and He longs to have close fellowship with you. More than anything He wants you to have an intimacy with God, close fellowship with Him, and a partnership with God in His kingdom work & mission.

God longs for you to spend time with Him daily and intimately communicate with Him, to hear His voice, to enjoy fellowship with Him, to trust and follow Him, and to join Him in His kingdom work. He wants to give your life great value and meaning and purpose through these things.

There are many reasons why you should pray and spend time with God. Here is why you should pray and regularly spend time with God:

#1 REASON: GOD DESIRES YOUR FELLOWSHIP:
- "God is faithful, through whom you were called into *fellowship* with His Son, Jesus Christ our Lord." - I Corinthians 1:9
- The Greek word for fellowship is "koinania" - this means the closest possible intimate fellowship with God, complete unity with God (being one with Him), and also having a partnership with God in His Kingdom work and mission.
- "You are all sons of God through faith in Christ Jesus." – Galatians 3:26
- " I no longer call you servants, because a servant does not know his master's business; I have called you friends..." – John 15:15
- See "Your Identity In Christ" (WHO YOU ARE IN CHRIST)

* GOD DESIRES FOR YOU TO KNOW HIM, TO BELIEVE HIM, TO UNDERSTAND THAT HE IS GOD.
- read John 17:3 ; Isaiah 43:10 ; Psalm 27:4
- Remember, God wants much more for you in your fellowship with Him than just to know about Him. God wants you to know Him in real & personal ways, by seeing and experiencing Him in and around your life. This is a much better & more intimate and real knowledge of God than just knowing about Him.

* BECAUSE JESUS IS THE SOURCE OF ABUNDANT & FULL LIFE:
- Deuteronomy 30:15-20; John 10:10, John 14:6 (GOD/ JESUS IS YOUR LIFE)
- Deuteronomy 8:3 (GOD'S WORD LEADS YOU TO ABUNDANT LIFE)
- Lamentations 3:24 (GOD IS THE SOURCE OF ALL YOU NEED & WANT)
- John 6:35; IS. 55:1-3 (ONLY JESUS CAN SATISFY & FULFILL YOU)
- John 8:12 (ONLY JESUS GIVES PURPOSE & DIRECTION FOR YOUR LIFE)
- Psalm 63:1-5 (NOTHING IS BETTER THAN INTIMACY WITH GOD)

What do you think of when you hear the words "abundant life"? Having a lot of material things? Having a lot of money? Living on a tropical island? Something else?
- In John 10:10 Jesus tells us that He came to give us life – eternal life forever in heaven, and abundant & meaningful life here on earth.
- John 14:6 Jesus tells us that "He is the life" – the source of eternal life & abundant life.
- You need to walk with Jesus in an intimate love relationship, daily trusting & obeying & following Him, in order to experience the full and abundant life only He can give.

You cannot have abundant and full life without Jesus. When you give yourself fully to Jesus, then He will fill you with His overflowing and abundant and victorious life – He is the life. "O, the fullness, the pleasure, the sheer excitement of knowing God on earth." – Jim Elliott

* YOU NEED TO SPEND TIME WITH GOD & BE FULLY COMMITTED TO HIM IN ORDER TO KNOW HIM INTIMATELY & TO BECOME LIKE JESUS.

- Philippians 3:8-10 - "What is more, I consider everything a loss because of the surpassing worth of knowing Christ Jesus my LORD, for whose sake I have lost all things. I consider them garbage, that I may gain Christ 9and be found in him, not having a righteousness of my own that comes from the law, but that which is through faith in Christ-the righteousness that comes from God on the basis of faith. 10I want to know Christ-yes, to know the power of his resurrection and participation in his sufferings, becoming like him in his death."

- Psalm 27:4 - "One thing I ask from the LORD, this only do I seek: that I may dwell in the house of the LORD all the days of my life, to gaze on the beauty of the LORD and to seek him in his temple."

- Like Paul & David, you need to be passionate in your seeking to know God, and in your fellowship with Him.

God's word promises us that when we seek God with all of our heart we will find Him. May we have a desire and passion in our hearts to spend time with God and seek Him.
- "Now devote your heart and souls to seeking the Lord your God." – I Chronicles 22:19
- "And you my son Solomon, acknowledge the God of your father, and serve him with wholehearted devotion and with a willing mind, for the Lord searches every heart and understands every motive behind the thoughts. If you seek Him he will be found by you; but if you forsake Him, He will reject you forever." – I Chronicles 28:9
- "For I know the plans I have for you, plans to prosper you and not to harm you, plans to give you hope and a future. Then you will call upon me and come and pray to me, and I will listen to you. You will seek me and find me when you seek me with all your heart. – Jeremiah 29:11-13

* GOD WANT YOU TO HUMBLE YOURSELF BEFORE HIM AND ACKNOWLEDGE HIM IN ALL THINGS. HE WANTS YOU TO DEPEND ON HIM.

- " Trust in the LORD with all your heart and lean not on your own understanding; 6in all your ways submit to him, and he will make your paths straight." - Proverbs 3:5-6

– also read Daniel 10:12, 2 Chronicles 7:14, I Peter 5:6, and Micah 6:8

"That which brings the praying soul near to God is humility of heart…Pride, self-esteem, and self-praise effectually shut the door of prayer." - E.M. Bounds

"I discovered an astounding truth: God is attracted to weakness. He can't resist those who humbly and honestly admit how desperately they need him. Our weakness, in fact, makes room for his power." - Jim Cymbala "Fresh Wind/ Fresh Fire"

God reveals Himself and His will and plans and His activity to people who humble themselves under Him, to people who fully acknowledge their complete & vital need for Him, to people who fully reverence Him and acknowledge that Jesus is Lord and Master and everything belongs to Him, and to people who out of love and reverence for Him fully yield and submit themselves to Him.

* IT IS GOD'S DESIRE & WILL FOR YOU TO PRAY AND TALK TO HIM CONTINUALLY, AND TRUST EVERYTHING IN YOUR LIFE TO HIM:

- "**pray** continually, give thanks in all circumstances; for this is God's will for you in Christ Jesus." - I Thessalonians 5:17-18

Since God is your loving Heavenly Father, He deeply cares for you (see I Peter 5:7) and about all the details of your life. He wants to help you to have the very best life you can. Trust Him and talk to Him about everything in your life, and turn it all over to Him.

* YOU NEED GOD'S GUIDANCE & WISDOM & POWER & STRENGTH & PROTECTION & PROVISIONS & COMFORT & PRESENCE IN OUR LIVES. **YOU NEED GOD**.

- Jeremiah 10:21, 23 - "The shepherds are senseless and do not inquire of the LORD; so they do not prosper and all their flock is scattered."

* YOU ARE IN A SPIRITUAL BATTLE AGAINST EVIL FORCES; YOU WILL LOSE THE BATTLE IF YOU FIGHT IN YOUR OWN POWER BECAUSE SATAN IS MORE POWERFUL THAN WE ARE. BUT GOD WILL GIVE YOU VICTORY DAILYIF YOU PRAY & WALK WITH HIM AND LET HIM FIGHT THE BATTLES.

- 1 Peter 5:8 - "Be alert and of sober mind. Your enemy the devil prowls around like a roaring lion looking for someone to devour."

- Daniel 10:12-13 - "Do not be afraid, Daniel. Since the first day that you set your mind to gain understanding and to humble yourself before your God, your words were heard, and I have come in response to them. 13But the prince of the Persian kingdom resisted me twenty-one days. Then Michael, one of the chief princes, came to help me, because I was detained there with the king of Persia."

- 1 John 4:4 - "You, dear children, are from God and have overcome them, because the one who is in you is greater than the one who is in the world."

- Matthew 26:40-41 - "Then he returned to his disciples and found them sleeping. "Couldn't you men keep watch with me for one hour?" he asked Peter. 41"Watch and pray so that you will not fall into temptation. The spirit is willing, but the flesh is weak."

- "For our struggle is not against flesh and blood, but against the rulers, against the authorities, against the powers of this dark world and against the spiritual forces of evil in the heavenly realms." – Ephesians 6:12, (also see v.18-20)

You need God to fight your battles for you, so that you can experience His victories in your life, and in your service for Him, and in your efforts to reach the lost people around you.

* BECAUSE YOUR CHILDREN & FAMILY NEED YOUR PRAYERS; HOW DO YOU KNOW HOW THEY'LL TURN OUT ? HOW DO YOU KNOW THAT THEY'LL STAY ON THE PATH THAT GOD HAS PLANNED FOR THEM AND CHOOSE TO LOVE HIM AND SERVE HIM ALL THEIR LIVES ?

- James Dobson, founder of Focus On The Family, tells the story of how his great great grandfather prayed for years that the next 4 generations in his family would all be Godly people and love and serve the Lord throughout their lives. Late in his life God assured him that this would happen. Every male in his family in the next 4 generations became a pastor, and every female became a pastor's wife. James Dobson went on to be the founder of Focus On The Family.

*BECAUSE YOU HAVE MUCH TO ACCOMPLISH ; YOU WILL ACCOMPLISH FAR MORE FOR GOD IN YOUR SERVICE, FAR MORE AT HOME, FAR MORE AT WORK,... IF YOU TURN IT OVER TO GOD FIRST, LET HIM RUN THE SHOW & LEAD YOU, AND LET **HIM** WORK THROUGH YOU.

- Isaiah 26:12 - "LORD, you establish peace for us; all that we have accomplished you have done for us."

- John 15:5 - "I am the vine; you are the branches. If you remain in me and I in you, you will bear much fruit; apart from me you can do nothing."
  - we will not be able to produce spiritual eternal fruit without the Lord empowering us and working through us

"Abide" or "remain" in Jesus means to **live in vital unity with Him**. You need to have an ongoing intimate relationship with Jesus in order to be a fruitful disciple of His, and to have the abundant and meaningful and fruitful life that God wants you to have.

" The supernatural power of God can accomplish far more than the combined fleshly efforts of sincere Christians." - Henry Blackaby / "Experiencing God"

"When we try to do the work of God in our own ways, we will never see the mighty power of God in what we do." - Henry Blackaby / "Experiencing God"

"LORD, the God of our ancestors, are you not the God who is in heaven? You rule over all the kingdoms of the nations. Power and might are in your hand, and no one can withstand you... Our God, will you not judge them? For we have no power to face this vast army that is attacking us. We do not know what to do, but our eyes are on you." - 2 Chronicles 20:6, 12

"The prayer of a righteous person is powerful and effective." - James 5:16b

"I can do all this through him who gives me strength." - Philippians 4:13

A right and intimate fellowship with God, and a heart that is committed to God and to prayer and the things of God is the key to having a full and fruitful and victorious life. When you fully surrender yourself to Jesus and let Him set the agenda for your life, then He is able to fill and control and direct you, and **He** will do everything with you and through you. When you decide to continually do this you will begin to see Jesus do immeasurably more than all you ask and imagine (see **Ephesians 3:20-21**), and God will be greatly glorified through your life.

* WHENEVER JESUS NEEDED TO KNOW GOD'S AGENDA AND THEN ACCOMPLISH IT, HE PRAYED. HE DID THIS DAILY:

Jesus gave you an excellent example you need to follow. In **John 5:19-20** and **30** Jesus said that apart from God's power he could do nothing. This shows that he was fully human during his life here on earth. He also said that he lived to do His Father's will and to please Him (also see **John 4:34**), because his motive for all he did was out of love for God. If Jesus needed to pray and seek God's agenda and plans, and then have to depend on God to provide the strength and power, then so will you. When you live in complete intimacy and unity with God, He will be able to accomplish supernatural things through you.

- John 14:10-12 - "The words I say to you I do not speak on my own authority. Rather, it is the Father, living in me, who is doing his work. Believe me when I say that I am in the Father and the Father is in me; or at least believe on the evidence of the works themselves. Very truly I tell you, whoever believes in me will do the works I have been doing, and they will do even greater things than these, because I am going to the Father.
- Luke 6:12-13 - "One of those days Jesus went out to a mountainside to pray, and spent the night praying to God. When morning came, he called his disciples to him and chose twelve of them, whom he also designated apostles."

* THE KEY TO TIME MANAGEMENT: (Charles Stanley) - Luke 6:12-19
"You won't find a Bible passage that says that Jesus rushed or ran. He never dashed to keep an appointment or scrambled to finish a task. He did exactly what He needed to do in just the right amount of time-- never early, never late. He was never too busy to meet unexpected needs. For a Savior with so much to do in so short a time, this unhurried approach may seem surprising. Three years was all He had to complete His ministry. And constantly the needy crowds were pushing to get to Him, desperately seeking His attention. What was His secret ? Jesus knew who sustained Him and kept Him on track. "He went off to the mountain to pray, and He spent the whole night in prayer to God."(v.12) It was God the Father who set His pace and directed every step. As a result, spending time with God was more important to Jesus than anything else. The next day He was refreshed and ready to begin the Sermon on the Mount. The key to Time Management is time spent with God. When you give God first place each day in prayer and reading his Word, He helps you discern what's important to Him and accomplish it on time. Are you letting God set your agenda ? His schedule is always best.

* BECAUSE YOUR NATION NEEDS PRAYER, AND NEEDS GOD TO MOVE IN PEOPLE'S HEARTS & LIVES. OUR NATION NEEDS GOD'S PEOPLE TO HUMBLE THEMSELVES, FERVENTLY PRAY & SEEK GOD AGAIN, AND TURN COMPLETELY AND WHOLEHEARTEDLY BACK TO HIM (2 Chronicles 7:13-14)

"Judgment in this life may be remedial, and bring you back to a right relationship with God, or final, displaying His wrath against your sin and leaving no opportunity for repentance. God can use natural disasters, human conflict, disease... to bring judgment. God's discipline seeks to lead you to cry for help, repent, and experience revival." -Henry Blackaby

Our nation desperately needs you (and all of God's people) to turn fully back to Him, to live the way God wants you to, and to fervently pray and intercede for your nation and the lost people in it. Your nation and world desperately need to see God pour out a spirit of revival in His people, and a spiritual awakening so that many many lost people will come to know Christ and avoid judgement.

HOW GOD SEES YOU (YOUR IDENTITY IN CHRIST)

You are dearly loved by God and a special treasure to Him. You are more valuable to Him than anything else that He has created, and He longs for you to have intimacy with God and close fellowship with Him.

You are a priceless masterpiece, and He is constantly at work in your life and circumstances to mold & shape you to be the best you can be.

Our identity is not based on what we have or what we do, even though society will try to tell you otherwise. Your identity is not based on your successes or failures. You identity in Christ is your true identity. Who God says you are in His Word is your true identity.

Here is your true identity in Christ:

1. GOD SEES YOU AS HIS BELOVED CHILD:
   - I JOHN 3:1,2
   - ROMANS 8:14-16
   - GALATIANS 3:26
   - EPHESIANS 5:2

2. JESUS CALLS YOU HIS FRIEND:
   - JOHN 15:14-15
   - PROVERBS 18:24
   - JAMES 2:21-24

3. GOD SEES YOU AS A SPECIAL TREASURE:
   - DEUTERONOMY 7:6
   - EXODUS 19:5
   - GENESIS 1:26

4. YOU ARE SPECIAL & PRECIOUS TO GOD:
   - ISAIAH 43:4
   - I PETER 2:9
   - PSALM 149:4;9

5. GOD LOVES YOU UNCONDITIONALLY (JUST AS YOU ARE):
   - ROMANS 5:8
   - ROMANS 8:38-39
   - I JOHN 3:16
   - PSALM 103:11-22

6. GOD ACCEPTS YOU UNCONDITIONALLY (JUST AS YOU ARE):
   - EPHESIANS 1:5
   - ROMANS 8:15

7. GOD CARES FOR YOU:
   - I PETER 5:7 (every detail, problem, need, hurt,... in your life)

8. GOD SEES YOU AS HIS WORKMANSHIP (A PRICELESS MASTERPIECE):
   - EPHESIANS 2:10

9. GOD SEES YOU AS HEIRS TO HIS KINGDOM:
   - ROMANS 8:17
   - GALATIANS 4:7

10. GOD ALSO SEES YOU AS:
    - THE LIGHT OF THE WORLD (MATTHEW 5:14)
    - THE SALT OF THE EARTH (MATTHEW 5:13)
    - THE RIGHTEOUS (2 CORINTHIANS 5:21)
    - NOT GUILTY (ROMANS 5:18-19) (I JOHN 1:9)
    - THE APPLE OF HIS EYE (PSALM 17:8)

    - YOU NEED TO SEE YOURSELF AS GOD SEES YOU.

    - A LOVE RELATIONSHIP WITH GOD IS YOUR HIGHEST CALLING, YOUR HIGHEST PRIVILEGE, AND YOUR HIGHEST STATUS.

    - YOUR WORTH AND VALUE ARE DETERMINED BY YOUR LOVE RELATIONSHIP WITH GOD, NOT BASED ON WHAT YOU HAVE OR DO.

"For God so loved the world that he gave his one and only Son, that whoever believes in him shall not perish but have eternal life." - John 3:16

WEEK 2 STUDY REVIEW (Pages 21-28)

q WHAT IS THE NUMBER 1 REASON THAT GOD WANTS YOU TO PRAY AND SPEND TIME WITH HIM ?
____ To grow spiritually　　　　____ Because it's good for us
____ To appear more spiritual　　____ To feel good about ourselves
____ To make us a better Christian　____ God desires your fellowship

q REVIEW PAGES 27-28 - HOW GOD SEES YOU ; IS THERE ANY TRUTH FROM GOD'S WORD ABOUT WHO YOU ARE IN CHRIST THAT YOU HAVE NOT FULLY ACCEPTED ? ASK GOD TO HELP YOU OR FREE YOU TO ACCEPT THE TRUTH OF WHO YOU REALLY ARE TO HIM. YOUR TRUE IDENTITY IS IN CHRIST.

q WHICH STATEMENT BEST DESCRIBES GOD'S CALLING ON YOUR LIFE:
____ God calls you to be His loyal friend, to accomplish whatever purposes He has for you.
____ God calls you to do great things for Him and become the best Christian you can be.

q WHICH STATEMENTS BEST DEFINE THE STATEMENT "GOD IS OUR LIFE" & "JESUS CAME TO GIVE ABUNDANT LIFE" (Deut. 30:15-20; 8:1-4; John 10:10,...)
____ God is the creator and sustainer of your physical life, and that is His main emphasis in working in your life.
____ You better obey God or He will take away your life.
____ God is the only true source of all that we want and need: physically, emotionally, spiritually; only He can truly & fully meet our needs and satisfy our souls, and give us the fulfilling and purposeful and valuable life that we desire.
____ Many, many Christians make the mistake of going after things they think will satisfy and fulfill them, instead of working on their relationship with God and trusting & allowing God to meet all of their needs and to place His desires on their heart, which lead to a fulfilling and satisfying and valuable life.

q WHY DOES GOD WANT YOU TO PRAY & ASK HIM, IF HE ALREADY KNOWS WHAT YOU NEED ? (CHOOSE THE BEST ONES) :
____ He wants you to humble yourself before Him and realize your need to depend on Him.
____ He wants you to learn that you can get anything you want from Him, as long as you ask nicely and ask enough times.
____ He wants you to see and experience Him and His goodness in real & personal ways, so that you can really know Him and know that He can be trusted.
____ He wants you to learn Jesus' way of praying/living: "not my will, but Your will be done"

q CHOOSE THE STATEMENTS THAT SHOW GOD'S WAYS OF DOING THINGS:
____ You choose how you want to serve Him and then pray for His power & blessings.
____ You make your very best effort, pray, and then trust Him with the results.
____ You seek first to have a close relationship with Him, and seek His will and plans.
____ You need to first find out what God wants to do in and through you, pray for His grace and strength to follow & obey and for Him to lead & empower you, and then join Him.

Get face to face with God and prayerfully review this week's material. Ask God to show you how you can be closer to Him and more one with Him.

HOW TO PURSUE INTIMACY WITH GOD

God's Word is the best source for finding how to pursue an intimate love relationship and fellowship and partnership with God. 2 Timothy 3:16-17 says that His Word is useful for correcting, rebuking (pointing out the error of your ways), and training in righteousness - which is how to have the best possible fellowship and partnership with Him. God desires the fullest possible intimacy with you, and He has not left you without instructions on how you can experience this wonderful intimacy.

IMPORTANT PARTS OF YOUR PRAYER & FELLOWSHIP TIME WITH GOD:
- PRAISE & WORSHIP & ADORE GOD
- READ GOD'S WORD
- MEDITATE ON THE WORD
- CONFESS YOUR SINS & BE RIGHT WITH GOD
- IT'S THE RELATIONSHIP !!!

- HEARING GOD'S VOICE (PIWG II)
- POWERFUL PRAYER: PRAY THE WORD (PIWG II)
- GOD WANTS TO BLESS YOU & MEET YOUR NEEDS (PIWG II)
- GOD WANTS TO SET YOU FREE (PIWG II)
- PRAYING FOR OTHERS (PIWG II)
- PRAYING FOR: PASTORS, CHURCH, NATION & LEADERS (PIWG II)
- GIVE THANKS !!! (PIWG II)

Besides learning how to get the most out of your prayer and fellowship time with God, you need to have the right heart attitude - a strong desire and craving and longing for God - not just for His blessings in your life, but for Him. God needs to become the greatest blessing & treasure in your life.

* PURSUE (SEEK & DESIRE) AN INTIMATE, RIGHT RELATIONSHIP WITH GOD
- Read Psalm 27:4, 63:1-5; Proverbs 21:21; Matthew 6:21,33

* YOU NEED THE HOLY SPIRIT'S HELP IN ORDER TO PRAY & LIVE THE WAY GOD WANTS US TO, AND TO HAVE A CLOSE RELATIONSHIP WITH HIM.

- " Lord teach us to pray." - Luke 11:1

- "No one knows the thoughts of God except the Spirit of God." - I Corinthians 2:9-12

* ONLY GOD CAN GIVE YOU THE DESIRE TO KNOW HIM, TO SPEND TIME WITH HIM IN PRAYER AND IN HIS WORD, AND TO SUBMIT/COMMIT TO HIM.

- "I will give them a heart to know me, that I am the LORD. They will be my people, and I will be their God, for they will return to me with all their heart." - Jeremiah 24:7

- "for it is God who works in you to will and to act in order to fulfill his good purpose." - Philippians 2:13

* COMMIT IN YOUR HEART TO SPEND TIME WITH GOD AND TO SEEK TO KNOW HIM BETTER, AND TO MAKE HIM YOUR 1ST LOVE AND TREASURE:

"LORD, GIVE ME A DESIRE TO SPEND TIME WITH YOU, TO KNOW YOU, TO PLEASE YOU, AND TO FOLLOW YOU."

Vital & Important Aspects For Intimate Fellowship with Jesus

There are many similarities between having a good marriage relationship with your spouse and having a good personal relationship with God. In the Bible, there is a lot of language that refers to marriage in describing a personal relationship with God. Those who receive and profess Jesus as their Lord & Savior are referred to as the "bride of Christ". In Jeremiah 2:2 God says "I remember the devotion of your youth, how as a bride you loved me and followed me through the desert"; in Jeremiah 3:14 God speaks to His people after they had left Him: "Return, faithless people, declares the Lord, for I am your husband" and in 3:20: "But like a woman unfaithful to her husband, so you have been unfaithful to Me." We are God's 1st love, and He wants to be our 1st love and have an intimate personal relationship with us.

" God who has **called** you into **fellowship** with his Son Jesus Christ our Lord is faithful."
- **I Corinthians 1:9**

"**Koinania**" fellowship: "the fullest possible **partnership** and **fellowship** with God, and with others in the church. **Intimate fellowship** with God and His Son Jesus produces this type of fellowship and unity in a church (and in a marriage & family). **Only God** can produce this genuine koinania fellowship, love, and unity. - Henry Blackaby

Here are some vitals to having wonderful & intimate fellowship with Jesus:

- **Commitment**   - Deuternonomy 5:7-9   - Revelation 2:2-5
   (Be Faithful)   - Psalm 100:5   - John 21:6
                        - I Chron. 28:9   - Acts 2:42 ("they **devoted** themselves...")

(the Greek word for devoted means to "latch on and refuse to let go"; they "latched on" to Jesus and fully committed themselves to Him)

God is fully devoted & committed to us, and His love is an unfailing, forever loyal love. He wants us to be fully devoted and committed to Him, and to love Him as He loves us. Would a marriage be very good if only 1 of the 2 people were totally committed to the other ? Our relationship with God will not be very good if we are not as committed to Him as He is to us

- **Love**   - Deuteronomy 6:5   - John 15:13   - I Tim. 1:12-14
  ("Agape" Love)   - 2 Cor. 5:9, 14-15   - Luke 9:23
                    - Galatians 2:20   - I John 5:3

The Greek word "agape" for Love means "unconditional & sacrificial love", which Jesus demonstrated when He suffered and died on the cross to pay for the sins of the ones He loved. God wants us to love Him and others in the same way He loves us.

- **Respect, Honor**   - Psalm 25:12-14   - Luke 11:1-2
  Reverance   - Psalm 100   - Acts 2:43, 47
                       - I Chron. 28:9   - I Samuel 2:30

God is worthy of our reverence, and the more we know Him the more we will reverence Him and be in awe of Him. The word Praise means to "place great value on someone", so when we praise God we are communicating how much we care for Him and value Him

- Trust	- Proverbs 3:5-6	- Psalm 91:1-2, 14-16
(Faith)	- Psalm 22:4-5	- Hebrews 11:6, 1
	- Psalm 62:5-8	- Isaiah 55:8-9

You simply cannot have a good, intimate relationship with God or with your spouse if you cannot trust.

- Communication (2 way):

- Speak (Prayer)	- Acts 1:14, 2:42,...	- I John 5:14-15
	- Colossians 4:2	- I Thessalonians 5:16-18
	- Matthew 7:7	
- Listen (God Speaks)	- John 10:10-11, 27	- I Samuel 3:10
	- I Kings 19:11-12	- Psalm 46:10
	- Ecclesiastes 5:1	- Luke 10:38-42; 11:28

God wants us to talk to Him about and involve Him in all aspects of our life, and have a lifestyle of prayer & talking to Him. Hearing God's voice is the most important part of our prayer time with Him. Good communication and learning to hear His "still small voice" is essential to knowing God and His attributes, His ways, His will, and His plans

- Time, Effort To Know	- John 17:3	- Luke 10:38-42
Each Other	- Exodus 33:13, 17-18	- Luke 6:12-13
	- Matthew 11:25-27	- Philippians 3:8, 10

When you love someone you want to know them more & more. It takes time & effort & desire & determination in order to get to know God... it is a lifelong process and a heart attitude... make knowing God your main desire and pursuit - nothing will please Him more. The more you know Jesus the more you will love Him, and trust Him, and delight in Him, and follow & obey Him

- Honesty	- Psalm 62:8	- Psalm 13; 22:1-2, 6-7, 14-15
	- I Samuel 1:10-16	- Psalm 51:2-4, 10-12

God wants you to "pour out your heart to Him" (Psalm 62:8), whatever it is you are feeling and going through, because He deeply cares for you. Note how David would be completely honest with God in some of the Psalms (Psalm 13, 22,...). God is always truthful with us, and He wants us to be truthful with Him

" Do you _____ take Jesus to be your Lord, Master, Savior, and Friend; to love, honor, cherish, and obey; for better or for worse, for richer or for poorer, in health or in sickness;

even in death never to part ?"

PRAISE AND WORSHIP THE LORD

You cannot have intimate, open, honest, transparent, 2-way communication with Jesus until you are able to block out all distractions and be fully and totally focused on Jesus. You need to be hungry and ready to hear His voice. Your heart needs to be ready and prepared to hear Him and then respond to whatever He tells you. You need to have a worshipful and soft and willing and trusting and obedient heart ... a heart that loves God fully. That is what a true worshipper of God is.

* GOD INHABITS THE PRAISES OF HIS PEOPLE; YOUR AWARENESS OF GOD'S PRESENCE AND YOUR FOCUS ON HIM IS MADE GREATER WHEN YOU PRAISE/WORSHIP HIM; YOU ARE SENSITIZED TO HIS PRESENCE.

- "But thou art holy, O thou that inhabits the praises of Israel." - Psalm 22:3
- "And surely I am with you always, to the very end of the age." - Matthew 28:20

* YOUR PRAYER TIME & EVERY DAY SHOULD BEGIN WITH PRAISE SO YOU CAN GET MORE **FOCUSED** ON GOD'S PRESENCE.

- Why do you think church services start with praise & worship ? First to express your love and adoration for God, and to glorify and please Him.
- The main reason should be so you can get your focus on Him.
- Once you are focused on God, then you can **reverently listen** to Him speaking to you
- Once you hear God speak, then obediently **respond** to Him.
- Ecclesiastes 5:1 - "Guard your steps when you go to the house of God. Go near to **listen** rather than to offer the sacrifice of fools, who do not know that they do wrong."
- God is not interested in our being good religious people, or in our giving a little money or some offering at church. He wants us to have a soft & pliable & moldable heart that is ready to reverently listen to Him and then obey and follow – no matter what He tells us to do.

"Being self centered blinds us to God and his love, and hinders the love relationship. We'll have a hard time trusting God, hearing God, obeying God, experiencing God, and knowing God."   - Experiencing God

It is natural for humans to be focused on self, and to be self-centered. We all need God to touch and change and cleanse our hearts so that we can stop being self-centered and become God-centered and Kingdom-centered and focused people.

* YOU CANNOT INTIMATELY COMMUNICATE WITH GOD UNTIL YOU'VE MADE **A CONNECTION** & YOU'RE **FOCUSED** ON HIS PRESENCE.

You cannot have good intimate communication until you first are ready and willing to hear what God has to say. You need to take your focus off of everything around you and fully focus on God. In order to hear God speak to you, you need to be ready and willing to hear Him and then follow and obey whatever He tells you or however He leads you. Listening is not merely hearing God speak, but **acting upon it**. (Review page 39 - True Worship of God ... notice that as you go down the list of what true worship of God is, it involves reverently listening to Him, and obeying Him, and ultimately surrendering and giving all of yourself to Him.

* PRAISE GIVES THE GLORY TO GOD, IT LIFTS OUR SPIRITS, AND IT SETS THE TONE FOR YOUR TIME WITH GOD AND YOUR WHOLE DAY.

- Once you realize who you are with, you are humbled, your heart is softened, and you are ready to listen to God.

- Exodus 33:13 - "If you are pleased with me, teach me your ways so I may know you and continue to find favor with you. Remember that this nation is your people."

- Isaiah 1:19-20 - "If you are willing and obedient, you will eat the good things of the land; but if you resist and rebel, you will be devoured by the sword."

- also read Isaiah 6:1-8

* ONCE YOU FOCUS ON GOD, YOU CAN ENJOY HIS PRESENCE

- Psalm 16:8-11 - "I keep my eyes always on the LORD. With him at my right hand, I will not be shaken. 9Therefore my heart is glad and my tongue rejoices; my body also will rest secure, 10because you will not abandon me to the realm of the dead, nor will you let your faithful one see decay. 11You make known to me the path of life; you will fill me with joy in your presence, with eternal pleasures at your right hand."

- Isaiah 26:3 - "You will keep in perfect peace those whose minds are steadfast ("whose minds are fixed on you"), because they trust in you."

- Psalm 25:15 - "My eyes are ever on the LORD, for only he will release my feet from the snare."

* PRAISE IS A "GARMENT" THAT COVERS & PROTECTS YOU FROM BITTERNESS, AND FROM COMPLAINING, AND FROM UNGRATEFULNESS, AND FROM A SPIRIT OF HEAVINESS:

- Isaiah 61:3 - ""... and a garment of praise instead of a spirit of despair."

* GOD WANTS YOU TO DEVELOP A **LIFESTYLE** OF WORSHIP AND PRAYER AND BEING THANKFUL:

- I Thessalonians 5:16-18 - "Rejoice always, 17pray continually, 18give thanks in all circumstances; for this is God's will for you in Christ Jesus."

You need develop a **lifestyle** of worship, prayer /communicating with God, and being thankful: the more you know God, the more you will worship & rejoice in Him, the more you will trust Him and want to talk to Him about everything in your life, and the more thankful you will be.

- "Rejoice in the LORD always. I will say it again: Rejoice! Let your gentleness be evident to all. The LORD is near. Do not be anxious about anything, but in every situation, by prayer and petition, with thanksgiving, present your requests to God. And the peace of God, which transcends all understanding, will guard your hearts and your minds in Christ Jesus." **-** Philippians 4:4-7

- "Through Jesus, therefore, let us continually offer to God a sacrifice of praise-the fruit of lips that openly profess his name. And do not forget to do good and to share with others, for with such sacrifices God is pleased." - Hebrews13:15-16

* GOD WANTS YOUR PRAISE & WORSHIP OF HIM TO BE GENUINE AND FROM A HEART OF TRUE LOVE & ADORATION FOR GOD:

- "Yet a time is coming and has now come when the true worshipers will worship the Father in the Spirit and in truth, for they are the kind of worshipers the Father seeks. God is spirit, and his worshipers must worship in the Spirit & in truth." - John 4:23-24

* TRY PRAISING GOD IN THE BAD TIMES THAT HAPPEN IN YOUR LIFE, NOT JUST DURING THE GOOD TIMES- IT WILL LIFT YOUR SPIRITS

- "And we know that in all things God works for the good of those who love him, who have been called according to his purpose.... to conform us to the image of His Son." - ROMANS 8:28-**29**

* **WORSHIP IS A REFLECTION OF YOUR RELATIONSHIP WITH GOD**.

* EXAMPLES OF PRAISING AND WORSHIPPING GOD:

- "TRUE WORSHIP OF GOD" (Page 37) - PRAISE GOD FOR HIS CHARACTER (p.18,19)
- READ A PSALM OF PRAISE TO GOD (Psalm 8, 19, 23, 46, 95, 100, 103, 148, 149, 150)

- READ A BIBLE PASSAGE OF PRAISE TO GOD (Luke 1:46-55 ; I Chronicles 29:11-13)
PRAISE AS A WEAPON

PRAISE comes from the Latin word "pretium", meaning price. Prize is a variation of this word. Originally it meant "to set a great price on". So when we praise God, we are placing a **great value** on Him and His acts. God sees us as His "treasured possession" (**Duet. 7:6, Exodus 19:5**), and He wants to be our **Treasure** and our **First Love**. (also see **Matthew 6:21, 33** , **Revelation 2:1-4**)

PRAISE FOR GOD IS COMMUNICATING WHO GOD IS, WHAT HE HAS DONE, AND WHAT HE CAN DO. PRAISE IS A WEAPON AGAINST EVIL & THE ENEMIES OF GOD:

1. **PRAISE HONORS GOD** – In Luke 11 Jesus taught us to begin prayer with praise in order to
honor and glorify God. Psalm 29:2 tells us to give God the glory that is due Him. Praise helps us
to focus on God, and who He is, and His greatness.

2. **PRAISE HELPS US FOCUS ON GOD** – Psalm 22:3 says that God inhabits the praises of His people. As we praise Him we raise up a throne or structure for Him to fill (2 Chron. 5:13). Praise sensitizes us to God's presence, and helps us take our focus off of ourselves and onto Him.

3. **PRAISE HELPS US TO KNOW GOD** – It helps us to focus on His character and His attributes. As we praise Him we rehearse our knowledge of Him, and we come to know Him as what we praise Him to be.

4. **PRAISE BREAKS THE ENEMY'S OPPRESSION** – In Acts 16:25,26 Paul and Silas praised God and the doors in the prison they were in were opened and they escaped. Praise lifts us out of oppression, and also helps us out of our self-centered ways.

5. **PRAISE CONFUSES THE FORCES OF EVIL** – The power of praise in battles is shown in 2 Chronicles 20, Psalm 8:2, and Psalm 149:5-9. Praise helps us to focus on God and realize our need for Him, and thus turn the battle over to Him. When we do this, God will then bring Victory. This makes Praise and Prayer and Dependence on God great weapons in Spiritual Battles.

> "And now my head will be lifted up above my enemies around me;
> and I will offer in His tent sacrifices with shouts of joy; I will sing,

yes, I will sing praises to the Lord" - Psalm 27:6

TRUE WORSHIP OF GOD

True worship is a **lifestyle** of heartfelt expression of love, devotion, and passion for Jesus: "Therefore I urge you brothers, in view of God's mercy, to offer your bodies as **living sacrifices**, holy and pleasing to God – this is your **spiritual act of worship**." - **Romans 12:1**

God's Word the Bible is full of examples of various forms of true worship of God:

GLORIFY, EXALT GOD	Deut. 10:17, Psalm 29:2, 99:5; I Chronicles 16:2
PRAISE GOD	Psalm 22:3 , Psalm 8, 19, 23, 46, 95, 100, 150
HONOR GOD	I Samuel 2:30 (Place great value on God)
REVERENCE FOR GOD	Psalm 95:6 , Nehemiah 8:6c
BLESS GOD	Psalm 100:4b , Psalm 31:21 , Nehemiah 8:6
GIVE THANKS TO GOD	Psalm 100:4 , I Thessalonians 5:16-18
REJOICE & ENJOY GOD	Philippians 4:4 , I Thes. 5:16-18 , 2 Cor. 6:4-10
VERBAL TESTIMONY	Nehemiah 8:6b , Psalm 66:16-20
REMEMBER GOD'S ACTS	Psalm 150:2 , Deuteronomy 5:15
SONGS OF WORSHIP	Psalm 100:2b , Psalm 66:4
WORSHIP MUSIC	Psalm 100:1 , Psalm 150:3-5
LIFT UP HANDS	Nehemiah 8:6b , Psalm 63:4
REVERENTLY READ GOD'S WORD	Nehemiah 8:3,5 ; Psalm 19:7-11
SERVE GOD WITH A RIGHT HEART	Psalm 100:2 , Colossians 3:23
SEEK TO KNOW GOD	Psalm 63:1-4 ,84:1-2 ; James 4:8 Phil. 3:7-11
HUMBLE YOURSELF	2 Chronicles 7:14 , Exodus 33:13 , I Peter 5:6
GIVE TO SUPPORT GOD'S WORK	Psalm 66:13-15 , Malachi 3
HONOR THE LORD'S DAY	Nehemiah 8:9 , Exodus 20:8-11
CELEBRATE GOD & JESUS	Nehemiah 8:10 , Luke 2:10

HAVE AN OBEDIENT LIFE　　　　Psalm 101:1-3 , I John 5:3 , John 14:15

JESUS IS YOUR FIRST LOVE　　Revelation 2:1-4

SURRENDER & GIVE YOURSELF　Matthew16:2-25 , Romans 12:1-2, Luke 9:23
AND YOUR LIFE TO GOD　　　　John 15:13-15, Galatians 2:20 , Philippians 1:21

PRAISING GOD IN YOUR LIFE

PRAISE GOD FOR:

HIS PRESENCE
HIS SON JESUS CHRIST
HIS HOLY SPIRIT
HIS WORD
HIS PRINCIPLES & LAWS
BEING KING & LORD OF ALL
HIS ANGELS
HIS ALWAYS BEING THE SAME
HIS HOLINESS
HIS MERCY
HIS GRACE
HIS FORGIVENESS
HIS SALVATION
HIS LOVING KINDNESS
HIS PATIENCE
HIS AWESOME POWER
HIS DELIVERANCE
HIS WISDOM
HIS PERFECT PLANS FOR YOU
HIS AWESOME CREATION
HIS PROTECTION
HIS PROVISIONS
HIS CARING
HIS EVERLASTING LOVE
HIS LISTENING
HIS DISCIPLINE
HIS ACTIONS & ANSWERS
HIS DELAYS
HIS "NO'S"
ALL YOUR TRIALS
ALL YOUR TALENTS
ALL YOUR POSSESSIONS
ALL YOUR VICTORIES
ALL YOUR GOOD TIMES
ALL YOUR BAD TIMES

PRAISE GOD FOR WHO HE IS

1. GOD IS THE CREATOR OF ALL THINGS:
* GENESIS 1,2

2. THERE ARE 3 PARTS OR PERSONS OF GOD:
* GOD THE FATHER (GENESIS 1:26)
* GOD THE SON (JESUS) (JOHN 1:1,14)
* GOD THE HOLY SPIRIT (GENESIS 1:26)

3. GOD OWNS ALL & RULES OVER ALL THINGS:
* I CHRONICLES 29:11 * PSALM 47:6,7 * PSALM 24:1

4. GOD IS SOVEREIGN & IN CONTROL:
* I CHRONICLES 29:11 * PSALM 118:24

5. GOD IS ALL POWERFUL:
* REVELATION 19:6 * I JOHN 4:4

6. GOD KNOWS ALL THINGS:
* I SAMUEL 2:3 * PSALM 44:21 * JOB 38-41

7. GOD SEES ALL THINGS (FROM BEGINNING TO END):
* GOD'S FOREKNOWLEDGE: ACTS 2:23 ; I PETER 1:2
* GOD PLANS & SEES ALL IN OUR LIVES: DUET. 31:8 ; JEREMIAH 29:11 ; PROV. 15:3

8. GOD'S WILL IS FAR WISER & BETTER THAN OUR OWN:
* ISAIAH 55:8,9 * PSALM 18:30

9. GOD'S TIMING-- HE IS NOT IN A HURRY:
* GOD CONTROLS WHEN THINGS WILL HAPPEN: ACTS 1:7
* GOD IS NOT BOUND BY TIME: II PETER 3:8

10. GOD'S PERFECT CHARACTER:

* GOD IS ALWAYS THE SAME HEBREWS 13:8
* GOD IS HOLY REVELATION 4:8
* GOD IS MERCIFUL PSALM 100:5 ; EPHESIANS 2:4
* GOD IS GRACIOUS ISAIAH 30:18 ; EPHESIANS 2:8,9
* GOD IS COMPASSIONATE ISAIAH 30:18 ; LAMENTATIONS 3:22
* GOD IS KIND PSALM 36:7
* GOD IS FORGIVING I JOHN 1:9
* GOD IS FAITHFUL LAMENTATIONS 3:23
* GOD WILL NEVER FAIL US DEUTERONOMY 31:8 ; HEBREWS 13:5
* GOD IS ALWAYS WITH US MATTHEW 28:20 ; JOSHUA 1:9

WEEK 3 STUDY REVIEW (Pages 31-42)

q PLACE A CHECK BESIDES SOME OF THE KEY THINGS WE NEED TO DO IN OUR PRAYER & FELLOWSHIP TIME WITH GOD:
___ Praise & Worship Him   ___ Hear from God and His word
___ Meditate on God and His word   ___ Confess and reconnect to God
___ Pray for others   ___ Try to get all you want
___ Pray for unsaved people   ___ Pray for Pastors & Leaders
___ Pursue your own desires   ___ Pursue and seek to know God

q ACCORDING TO MATTHEW 6:33 & PROVERBS 21:21, WHAT IS THE KEY TO HAVING ALL YOU NEED, AND TO FINDING TRUE ABUNDANT LIFE:
___ Pray, Pray, Pray for the things you think will satisfy and fulfill you
___ Work very hard for the best things that life has to offer
___ Put your relationship with God first, and seek & pursue Him & His will & kingdom

q CHOOSE THE STATEMENTS THAT ARE TRUE:
___ People naturally have a heart to know God.   ___ All Christians are hungry for God.
___ People naturally want to live by God's will. ___ We need God's Spirit to help & guide us.
___ Christians automatically know God's will.   ___ We need God to cleanse us & change us.
___ We need to learn how to walk with God in order to be close & right with Him.

q YOU SHOULD START YOUR TIME WITH GOD & YOUR DAY WITH PRAISE:
___ To practice for Sunday services ___ To get your mind & heart focused on God
___ To butter him up & get all you want ___ To get focused so you can hear from God
___ To glorify and honor God ___ To get your focus off of self
___ To have a soft, humble, listening heart ___ To protect you from a spirit of despair

q WHY DOES GOD WANT US TO REJOICE IN HIM ALWAYS: (I Thes.5:16; Phil.4:4)
___ Because He has a "God-sized" ego and can't get enough compliments
___ Because it is pleasing to Him   ___ To help raise your perspective
___ Because God wants us to get to know Him and walk with Him, the only source of true joy and peace, so we can be filled with His joy and peace. (see John 14:21-27; 15:9-11)
___ Because it helps us get to know Him as what we praise Him for (see page 11, # 2)

q THE MORE YOU TRULY KNOW GOD, THE MORE NATURAL AND HEARTFELT YOUR PRAISING AND WORSHIP OF GOD WILL BE.

q IN WHAT WAYS IS PRAISING GOD ACTUALLY A SPIRITUAL WEAPON (Page 37):
___ Praise honors & glorifies God ___ You appear more spiritual as you do it
___ Praise helps you to know God better ___ Others will admire you for doing it
___ Praise sensitizes us to God's presence ___ Praise lifts us out of despair & oppression
___ Praise disarms & confuses the enemy ___ We are encouraged & strengthened when we sense He is near us

q REVIEW PAGES 39 & 40 - ARE YOU A TRUE WORSHIPPER & FOLLOWER OF JESUS ?

Get face to face with God and prayerfully review this week's material. Ask God to show you how you can be closer to Him and more one with Him.

READ GOD'S WORD (HEAR GOD'S VOICE)

Hearing God's voice is the most important part of your prayer & fellowship time with God, and is vital to your walk with Him. You cannot have intimate fellowship with Him and become one and a partner with God in His great Kingdom work if you do not reverently listen to Him and then follow Him as He leads and speaks. In John 10:4 & 27 Jesus tells us that His "sheep" or true followers know His (the Good Shepherd) voice and they follow Him. You cannot truly know and follow Jesus unless you can hear His voice, and unless He reveals Himself and His ways and His will & plans to you.

* GOD SPEAKS TO YOU THROUGH HIS WORD; HE REVEALS MUCH ABOUT HIMSELF, ABOUT HIS WILL & PLANS, HIS WAYS, HOW TO PLEASE HIM, AND ABOUT LIFE THE WAY HE INTENDED IT TO BE. (Read Exodus 33:13-34:11)

Exodus 33:11 tells us that God spoke to Moses face to face, as one speaks to a friend. Verses 13-18 show us that Moses had a humble & seeking & hungry heart (hungry for God), and because of his heart for God, God was able to reveal Himself and His glory to Moses. Moses also faithfully served and followed God, however God would lead.

* READING GOD'S WORD THIS EARLY IN YOUR QUIET TIME ALLOWS GOD TO SPEAK TO YOU & HAVE FIRST PLACE IN YOUR QUIET TIME WITH HIM

Read I Samuel 3:9-10 ... your heart attitude needs to be "speak Lord, your servant is listening." The
Biblical word for listen means to "reverently listen to God, with the intent of doing or following whatever you hear - even before you hear it. Is this your heart attitude ?

* "IMMERSE YOURSELF IN GOD'S WORD -- IT IS YOUR LIFE"
- Deuternonmy 8:3 and 30:15-19
- John 10:10, 14:6
- Remember, God wants you to have the fullest, most satisfying & fulfilling life. Never forget that without close fellowship with Jesus, you cannot have abundant life. God wrote His word personally to you, so that you, His dearly loved child,would follow Him & have abundant life.

* READING THE WORD OF GOD ALLOWS YOU TO GROW SPIRITUALLYCLOSER TO HIM, ONE WITH HIM & HIS WILL & PLANS, AND MORE LIKE JESUS - FILLED WITH HIS LIFE, HIS POWER, HIS VICTORY, HIS GLORY,...

Read 2 Timothy 3:16-17 ... God gave you His word to teach you, to correct and transform you, and to train and help you to seek and obtain the fullest and closest fellowship and partnership with Him. It is His primary way of speaking to you and instructing you, and to help make you the best you can be - which is to become more and more like Jesus.

- "... LIKE NEWBORN BABIES, CRAVE PURE SPIRITUAL MILK, SO THAT BY IT YOU MAY GROW UP IN YOUR SALVATION." - I Peter 2:2

*THE WORD OF GOD TEACHES YOU TRUTH:

In John 14:6 Jesus tells you that He is the Way, He is the Truth, and He is the Life. Because Jesus is Truth, anything He tells you is the truth. You need to spend time with the Truth so that you will know truth, especially spiritual truth. Then you will never be misled and will be able to discern what is truth and what is not truth.

"SANCTIFY THEM BY THE TRUTH; YOUR WORD IS TRUTH." - JOHN 17:17

* JESUS SAID, "IF YOU HOLD TO MY TEACHING (IF YOU CONTINUE IN MY WORD), YOU ARE REALLY MY DISCIPLES. THEN YOU WILL KNOW THE TRUTH (JESUS), AND THE TRUTH (JESUS)WILL SET YOU FREE." - John 8:31-32

What do you need to be set free from ? Do you need to be set free from fear ? Anxiety ? Worry ? Deception & lies ? Insecurity ? Depression ? Discouragement ? Sin ? Something else ? Run to Jesus and His Word - He wants to set you to know Him- Truth, and He wants to set you free !!!

* THE WORD OF GOD HELPS PURIFY YOUR HEART & MIND, AND TO TRANSFORM YOU TO BE MORE LIKE JESUS (READ 2 Corinthians 3:8):

- "... CHRIST LOVED THE CHURCH, & GAVE HIMSELF UP FOR HER TO MAKE HER HOLY, CLEANSING HER BY THE WASHING WITH WATER THROUGH THE WORD ...
- Ephesians 5:25-26

- "... DO NOT CONFORM ANY LONGER TO THE PATTERN OF THIS WORLD, BUT BE TRANSFORMED BY THE RENEWING OF YOUR MIND."   - Romans 12:1,2

- " HOW CAN A YOUNG MAN KEEP HIS WAY PURE ? BY **LIVING** ACCORDING TO YOUR WORD."   - Psalm 119:9

God wants you to be a special and holy person of glory, completely set apart from evil and the things of the world. He also wants you to become the very best person you can be, which in God's definition is to become more and more like Jesus. Holy like Jesus; loving like Jesus, joyful like Jesus, kind like Jesus, patient like Jesus, faithful to God like Jesus, passionate about God like Jesus, passionate about reaching the lost like Jesus (see Luke 19:10 and Matthew 4:19),...

* GOD ENCOURAGES & ASSURES YOU THROUGH HIS WORD:

> "The only way to remove the fear from our lives is to listen to
> God's assurances to us in His Word." - Oswald Chambers

Since God is Truth, His Word and His promises are all truth. When you let God speak to you early in your prayer time and early in your day, He will bless you and encourage you through His word.

* THE WORD OF GOD GIVES YOU A WEAPON BY WHICH YOU CAN FIGHT OFF SATAN AND HIS ATTACKS AND HIS LIES.

In Matthew 4 Jesus fights temptation and lies by the enemy and wins by quoting Scripture 3 times. Jesus gives you the perfect example of how to fight against and win over temptation, lies, and deceit, which are some of Satan's primary tools to get you away from God and in bondage and defeat.

* GOD'S WORD TEACHES YOU AND GUIDES YOU DOWN THE PATHS HE HAS PLANNED FOR YOUR LIFE: (GOD KNOWS & WANTS WHAT IS BEST FOR YOU)
"YOUR WORD IS A LAMP TO MY FEET, & A LIGHT FOR MY PATH." - Psalm 119:105

- also read Psalm 16:8-11 , Isaiah 48:17-18 , and Jeremiah 29:11-13

* GOD'S LAWS & PRINCIPLES PROTECT YOU AND ARE FOR YOUR GOOD:

- "THE PRECEPTS OF THE LORD ARE RIGHT, GIVING JOY TO THE HEART." - Psalm 19:8

- "THIS IS LOVE FOR GOD: TO OBEY HIS COMMANDS. AND HIS COMMANDS ARE NOT BURDENSOME." - I John 5:3

* THE POSITIVE EFFECTS OF LIVING BY GOD'S WORD: Psalm 19:7-11

As your loving Heavenly Father, God cares deeply for you and wants to protect you from anything that can be harmful to you. He wrote His Word out of love for you, to protect you, to guide you, to bless you. I John 5:3 reveals the proof of whether you and I truly living out of love for God - reverence and trust and obedience to Him and His Word.

* READ GOD'S WORD AS IF YOU ARE DIGGING FOR **GREAT TREASURES**:

-"WITH MY LIPS I RECOUNT ALL THE LAWS THAT COME FROM YOUR MOUTH. I REJOICE IN FOLLOWING YOUR STATUTES AS ONE REJOICES IN **GREAT RICHES**."

- read Psalm 119:13,14

- also read Matthew 11:25-27; 13:10-12 , Proverbs 25:2 , Isaiah 43:22 and 64:6-7

Don't miss the great truth that the **treasure** you are digging for in God's Word is God Himself. When you can truly say that Jesus is your **treasure** and the most valuable person by far in your life, then you
are truly living in a passionate love affair with Jesus and you are truly living.
  ·

* FROM HOWARD HENDRICKS: "LIVING BY THE BOOK":
- READ THE BIBLE AS IF IT WERE A **LOVE LETTER FROM GOD**.

- OBSERVATION, INTERPRETATION, APPLICATION (You cannot correctly **Apply** God's Word in your life unless you correctly **Interpret** it, and you cannot correctly Interpret His Word unless you **Examine & Observe** all that you possibly can)

- ASK QUESTIONS: Who, What, Where, When, Why, What now ? when you read

- LOOK FOR THINGS THAT ARE:
  - Emphasized (Jesus saying "truly truly",...)
  - Repeated over and over again
  - Related ("if ... then", "therefore",...)
  - Alike
  - Unalike
  - True to life (real life & real people)

God sent His Son Jesus to suffer & die for you, out of a great love for you. God sent His Word the Bible to you out of great love for you also. Always read God's Word as a Love Letter from God, and always read it as though God is **personally speaking to you** (put your name in the verses).

* REMEMBER, YOU'RE SPENDING TIME WITH A PERSON, NOT A BOOK OF LAWS OR A RELIGIOUS BOOK

* PERSONALIZE GOD'S WORD SO THAT IT FITS YOUR SPECIFIC CIRCUMSTANCES.

* READ GOD'S WORD ALOUD, AS THOUGH GOD HIMSELF IS TALKING TO YOU.

HOW WE MIGHT LOOK WHEN WE DON'T FOLLOW GOD'S DIRECTIONS IN HIS WORD

"Your word is a lamp to my feet, and a light for my path."
- Psalm 119:105

"The waywardness of the simple will kill them, and the complacency of fools will destroy them; but whoever listens to me will live in safety and be at ease, without fear of harm." - Proverbs 1:32-33

MEDITATE ON GOD'S WORD

* DON'T JUST QUICKLY READ GOD'S WORD... EXAMINE IT THOROUGHLY AND REFLECT ON WHAT GOD IS SAYING:

- "**Reflect** on what I am saying, for the Lord will give you insight into all of this." - 2 TIM. 2:7
- "Now the Bereans were of more noble (honorable) character than the Thessalonians, for they **received the message** with **great eagerness** and **examined** the Scriptures every day to see if what Paul said was true." - ACTS 17:11

1. "**GOD, WHAT ARE YOU TRYING TO SAY TO ME ?**" (1 Samuel 3:10)
- IS THERE SIN TO AVOID ?
- IS THERE A PROMISE TO CLAIM ?
- IS THERE A COMMAND TO OBEY ?
- IS THERE A BLESSING TO ENJOY ?
- IS THERE AN EXAMPLE TO FOLLOW ?
- IS THERE SOMETHING NEW TO LEARN ABOUT GOD'S CHARACTER ?

2. "**HOW DOES WHAT I AM SENSING IN MY PRAYER TIME, OR MY CIRCUMSTANCES, OR WHAT GODLY PEOPLE ARE TELLING ME CONFIRM THIS ?**"

3. "**HOW CAN I DO THIS/ APPLY THIS/ FOLLOW THIS IN MY LIFE ?**"
- "Do not merely listen to the word, and so deceive yourselves. **Do** what it says... But the man who looks **intently** into the perfect law that gives freedom, and continues to do this, not forgetting what he has heard, but doing it - he will be blessed in all he does." - JAMES 1:22,25

* MEMORIZE GOD'S WORD & TREASURE IT & KEEP IT IN YOUR HEART.
"I have hidden (treasured) your word in my heart that I might not sin against you."
- Psalm 119:11

* KEEP A SPIRITUAL JOURNAL AND WRITE DOWN THE VERSES AND WHAT GOD SAYS TO YOU OR TELLS YOU TO DO.

* CLOSE YOUR EYES & MEDITATE ON GOD AND ON HIS WORD
- read Psalm 111:2-4
- meditate on Isaiah 40:12 and Isaiah 49:15,16

* WHEN GOD SPEAKS THROUGH HIS WORD, LISTEN TO HIM & OBEY.

- read Psalm 1:2-3 and Deuteronomy 5:32-33
- "Do not let this book of the law depart from your mouth; **meditate on it day and night**, so **that** you may **be careful** to **do** everything written in it. **Then** you will be **prosperous** and **successful**." Joshua 1:8

ARE YOU SUCCESSFUL ?

God wants you to be a blessed, fruitful, and successful person.

What is success ? Most people define success in terms of achieving goals, acquiring wealth, and having prestige, favor, status, and power. "Successful" people enjoy the "good life" – being financially secure, emotionally secure, being surrounded by admirers, and enjoying the fruits of their labor.

Their example is emulated and their accomplishments are noticed. Most people's definitions of success only deal with the "here and now" of this life. Even in many churches today the definition of success is in terms of numbers, size, dollars and prestige.

But success is measured and defined differently by God. God's measure of success involves our **obedience** and **faithfulness** to Him, regardless of opposition and personal cost. His measure of success is whether or not we are being loyal to Him in our personal relationship with Him and in our life, and whether we are accomplishing His goals & purposes for our life.

Some examples in the Bible:

Jeremiah was an absolute failure when judged by people's definition of success. For 40 years he served as God's spokesman, but when he spoke no one listened and responded. He was rejected by his neighbors, his family, the priests and prophets, friends, his audiences, and the kings. He was poor and underwent severe deprivation to deliver God's messages. He was thrown into prison and into a cistern. But in God's eyes he was a success. He faithfully and courageously proclaimed God's word and His messages, and he was obedient to his calling.

Jesus was also a failure, if you measure his life here on earth by people's measure of success. He had little in material possessions, and did not even own a home. He was rejected by most people, and was even hated by some. The religious leaders of the time despised him. Even his friends and those closest to him deserted him.

- He was accused and found guilty of things he did not do. He was beaten, spit on, cursed, mocked, and he suffered terribly and died the most horrible kind of death known to man at that time, death on the cross. Measure him by the way most of us measure success, and he was a failure.

- But in God's eyes, the redemption and salvation of all of mankind was accomplished through His son Jesus. By God's grace and great love for you and I, He sent Jesus to pay for our sins, and now the gift of a restored personal relationship with God and eternal life can be ours – all because of Jesus Christ.

"God's call is for you to be his loyal friend, to accomplish His purposes and goals for your life" – Oswald Chambers

"Do not let this book of the Law depart from your mouth; meditate on it day and night, so that you may be careful to do everything written in it. Then you will be prosperous and successful." – God (Joshua 1:8)

"He who pursues righteousness (close & right fellowship with God) and love, finds life, prosperity, and honor." – God (Proverbs 21:21)

"Such confidence as this is ours through Christ before God. Not that we are competent in ourselves… but our competence comes from God. He has made us competent as ministers of a new covenant…" – 2 Corinthians 3:4-6

Success is measured and defined differently by God. God's measure of success involves our **obedience** and **faithfulness** to Him, regardless of opposition and personal cost. His measure of success is whether or not we are being loyal to Him in our personal relationship with Him and in our life, and whether we are accomplishing His goals & purposes for our life.

WEEK 4 STUDY REVIEW (Pages 45-52)

q CHOOSE THE BEST DESCRIPTIONS OF WHAT READING GOD'S WORD IS:
____ It is a big part of having intimate communication with God.
____ It is meant to be a religious exercise designed to make you a better Baptist or Methodist...
____ It is the Living God ("the Living Word") speaking personally to you.
____ It is good for you to do, so you can show off your knowledge of the Bible.
____ It is God revealing Himself, His ways to closely walk with Him and please Him, His plans and promises for your life and future,...

q CHOOSE THE BEST MEANINGS OF THE PHRASE "SPIRITUAL GROWTH":
____ It means that you have amassed a great deal of intellectual knowledge of the Bible.
____ It means you are growing closer to God, more one with Him, and more like Jesus.
____ It means that you are growing in your trust, love, devotion, and passion for God.
____ It means that God has been able to reveal more and more about Himself and His ways and plans to you, along with the deeper truths of His word, because you have a humble, soft, seeking, teachable heart.

q GOD'S WORD TEACHES US TRUTH (JESUS IS THE TRUTH -- JOHN 14:6), AND THAT THE TRUTH WILL SET US FREE (JOHN 8:31,32). HERE ARE SOME THINGS PEOPLE NEED TO BE SET FREE FROM:
* Eternal Separation from God * Spiritual Strongholds / Lies or Deceptions
* Insecurity * Unforgiveness
* Fear, Worry, Anxiety * Discouragement
* Legalism * Self Effort / Self Sufficiency
* Bitterness * Pride

q MARK SOME OF THE OTHER PURPOSES & BENEFITS OF GOD & HIS WORD:
___ God's Word purifies our hearts & minds ___ He helps transform us to be more like Jesus
___ He encourages & comforts & assures us ___ He gives us a weapon against Satan's lies
___ He gives us principles for our own good ___ It leads us to abundant life (He IS the Life)

q MARK T FOR TRUE OR F FOR FALSE:
____ You should read God's word as if it were a book of laws & religious rules.
____ You should read God's word is if you were digging for **hidden treasure**.
____ You should read God's word as a **love letter** to you from your loving Father.
____ Most people are naturals when it comes to observing all God is saying in the Bible.
____ You have to learn how to observe all you can before you can correctly interpret it.
____ If you incorrectly interpret what God is saying, you will correctly apply it to your life.
____ You don't need the Holy Spirit to help you reveal what God is saying to you personally.

q PERSONALIZING GOD'S WORD TO FIT YOUR CIRCUMSTANCES MEANS:
___ You twist or change His word so that it says what you really want it to say.
___ You take your life & circumstances to God's word and see what He has to say about it, and then you adjust your thinking and actions accordingly.
___ Also, read God's word as if God is speaking personally to you (put your name in the verses)

CHOOSE THE CORRECT ASPECTS OF MEDITATING ON GOD & HIS WORD:

____ You try to determine what God is saying to you by studying His word, contemplating it and thinking on it so it really sinks in, and by asking questions.
____ You talk to God about His word and ask Him to reveal to you what He is saying.
____ You take a yoga class so that you can learn eastern religion meditation.
____ You learn to be sensitive to God's Holy Spirit and learn to sense what He places in your heart, especially during your prayer and fellowship time with Him.
____ You learn to ask "What does or should this look like in my life" or "How can I do this"
____ After you sense what God is saying, you go off into your day feeling more spiritual because you heard God speaking to you or leading you, and you leave it at that.
____ True and effective meditating on God and His word takes you from hearing from God through His word to applying & doing it in your life. This is loving & following God.

q GOD'S WORD TELLS US THAT IF WE ARE CAREFUL TO FOLLOW HIM & HIS WORD, WE WILL BE PROSPEROUS & SUCCESSFUL (Joshua 1:8). GOD'S DEFINITION OF SUCCESS & PROSPERITY INCLUDES THE FOLLOWING:
____ You will get the finest of houses and cars and clothes,...
____ God measures success & prosperity in terms of obedience and faithfulness to Him.
____ Your ministry for Him will be successful in the ways people measure success: large numbers of people, large fancy buildings, prestige and status among Christians,...
____ Your relationship with God will be increasingly closer and more intimate, you will grow more one with Him, and the abundant joy & peace & life of Jesus will fill your soul.
____ God will mold and shape your heart & character to be more and more like Jesus, and it will be hard to tell you apart from Jesus when God is finished with you.

q READ **LUKE 9:23**; **PRAYERFULLY MEDITATE** ON THIS VERSE EVERY DAY THIS WEEK AND ASK YOURSELF "WHAT SHOULD **FOLLOWING JESUS** LOOK LIKE IN MY LIFE ?" ; WRITE DOWN YOUR ANSWERS BELOW:
- I should pray & spend time with God every morning, like Jesus did.
- I should seek God's will and agenda ahead of my own, like Jesus did.
-
-
-
-
-
-
-

Get face to face with God and prayerfully review this week's material. Ask God to show you how you can be closer to Him and more one with Him.

CONFESS YOUR SINS/ RECONNECT TO GOD

Even though you have accepted Jesus Christ as your Lord and Savior and have His Holy Spirit living in you, there is still a battle against sin and temptation and the old sin nature. Since God is a holy and just God, He must turn away from sin. He absolutely cannot tolerate it or dwell near it. This is why it is absolutely critical for you to regularly maintain your fellowship with Jesus and to work on your relationship with Him. Since no one is perfect and all still sin, God has given you a way to be forgiven and washed from your sins, and to reconnect with Him and re-establish your fellowship with Him.

- "SEARCH ME, O GOD, AND KNOW MY HEART; TEST ME, AND KNOW MY ANXIOUS THOUGHTS. SEE IF THERE IS ANY OFFENSIVE WAY IN ME, AND LEAD ME IN THE WAY EVERLASTING." - Psalm 139:23,24

* LET GOD SEARCH FOR HIDDEN SINS & MOTIVES & HABITS THAT YOU ARE NOT EVEN AWARE OF. - Psalm 139:1-6

- "THE LORD SEARCHES EVERY HEART AND UNDERSTANDS EVERY MOTIVE BEHIND THE THOUGHTS." - I Chronicles 28:9

It is important to realize that no one - not even yourself - knows you and sees everything in your heart like God does. He knows your every thought, and He knows every motive behind every action of yours. Let God search you and reveal the things that are not pleasing to Him and the sin in your life, so that you can continue to enjoy all the benefits of having intimate fellowship with Jesus.

* YOU MUST HAVE A PURE HEART AND A RIGHT FELLOWSHIP WITH GOD
IN ORDER TO SEE AND KNOW GOD INTIMATELY:

- "BLESSED ARE THE PURE IN HEART, FOR THEY WILL SEE GOD." - Matthew 5:8

- "THE LORD IS FAR FROM THE WICKED; BUT HE HEARS THE PRAYER OF THE RIGHTEOUS". - Proverbs 15:29

- Review Page 29 - A Pure Heart

* IF YOUR PRAYERS ARE NOT BEING ANSWERED, DON'T BLAME GOD. SIN BREAKS YOUR FELLOWSHIP WITH GOD AND DISARMS YOUR PRAYERS:

- "BUT YOUR INIQUITIES HAVE SEPARATED YOU FROM GOD; YOUR SINS HAVE HIDDEN HIS FACE FROM YOU, SO THAT HE WILL NOT HEAR." - Isaiah 59:2

God wants to answer your prayers, and He promises to do so in many places in His Word (see Jeremiah 33:3, Matthew 7:7,...). When you allow sin in your heart and life, your personal fellowship with God is broken and thus your prayer life is disarmed. It is vital to maintain a right fellowship with God in order to see answers to your prayers, and to enjoy the abundant and victorious life that can only come through having unbroken fellowship with Jesus.

* YOU NEED TO REALIZE THAT YOUR SIN IS PERSONALLY AGAINST GOD:

"AGAINST YOU, YOU ONLY, HAVE I SINNED & DONE EVIL IN YOUR SIGHT."
- Psalm 51:4

* GOD WANTS YOU TO HAVE THE RIGHT HEART ATTITUDE: TRULY SORRY YOU SINNED AGAINST HIM, AND TO HAVE A REPENTANT HEART:

- read PSALM 51:10; 16-17
- review Page (Is Jesus Your 1st Love ? / Idols In Today's World)

God strongly and deeply loves you in a very personal way, so when you sin He sees it as a sin against Him and He takes it personally. Always remember that you are not sinning against a set of rules or regulations, or against religious rights and wrongs - your sin is personally against God. This truth and the fact that your personal fellowship with Jesus is broken should cause you to truly be sorry for your sin and to hopefully cause you to run to God, confess (agree with Him) your sin, and turn away from the sin or sin habit and turn back towards God.

* YOU ARE ASSURED THAT IF YOU CONFESS YOUR SINS YOU WILL BE FORGIVEN (GOD WANTS YOU TO TURN AWAY FROM THE SIN AND TURN TO HIM)

"IF WE CONFESS OUR SINS, HE IS FAITHFUL AND JUST AND WILL FORGIVE US OUR SINS AND PURIFY US FROM ALL UNRIGHTEOUSNESS."   - I John 1:9

– also read Isaiah 43:25 , Psalm 103:12 , Proverbs 28:13

"**REPENT** THEN, AND **TURN TO GOD**, SO THAT YOUR SINS MAY BE WIPED OUT, THAT TIMES OF REFRESHING MAY COME FROM THE LORD." - Acts 3:19

Repent- A change of mind, or a turning in another direction. A turning back to God.

Confessing means that you agree with God that you have sinned personally against Him, and that you are sorrowful that you have done so. So sorrowful in fact, that you decide in your heart to fully turn away from the sin against God and turn fully back to God and to living to please Him. When you do not turn back from the sin or sin habit and continue to sin against God, then He will as a loving Father do whatever is necessary to get you to decide to turn back to Him. God's discipline can be avoided. God will do whatever is necessary to get your attention and to get you to want to turn back to your fellowship with Him, because He so strongly loves you and wants the best for you.

COMMON PRAYER & RELATIONSHIP HINDRANCES

1. UNCONFESSED SIN:
- "IF I REGARD WICKEDNESS IN MY HEART, THE LORD WILL NOT HEAR." Psalm 66:18

2. LACK OF FAITH (James 1:6-7):
- "BUT WHEN HE ASKS, HE MUST BELIEVE & NOT DOUBT, BECAUSE HE WHO DOUBTS IS LIKE A WAVE OF THE SEA, BLOWN & TOSSED BY THE WIND. THAT MAN SHOULD NOT THINK HE WILL RECEIVE ANYTHING FROM THE LORD."

3. WILLFUL DISOBEDIENCE:
- "DEAR FRIENDS, IF OUR HEARTS DO NOT CONDEMN US, WE HAVE CONFIDENCE BEFORE GOD & RECEIVE FROM HIM ANYTHING WE ASK, BECAUSE WE OBEY HIS COMMANDS & DO WHAT PLEASES HIM."   - I John 3:21-23

4. LACK OF TRANSPARENCY WITH GOD & OTHERS:
- "THEREFORE, CONFESS YOUR SINS TO ONE ANOTHER AND PRAY FOR ONE ANOTHER, SO THAT YOU MAY BE HEALED. THE PRAYER OF A RIGHTEOUS MAN IS POWERFUL AND EFFECTIVE."   - James 5:16

5. UNFORGIVENESS:
- "FOR IF YOU FORGIVE MEN WHEN THEY SIN AGAINST YOU, YOUR HEAVENLY FATHER WILL ALSO FORGIVE YOU. BUT IF YOU DO NOT FORGIVE MEN THEIR SINS, YOUR FATHER WILL NOT FORGIVE YOUR SINS." - Matthew 6:14-15

6. WRONG / SELFISH MOTIVES (James 4:3):
"WHEN YOU ASK, YOU DO NOT RECEIVE, BECAUSEYOUASKWITHWRONGMOTIVES."

7. IDOLS IN OUR LIVES (See Page 26):
- "SON OF MAN, THESE MEN HAVE SET UP IDOLS IN THEIR HEARTS AND PUT WICKED STUMBLING BLOCKS BEFORE THEIR FACES. SHOULD I LET THEM INQUIRE OF ME AT ALL ?"   - Ezekiel 14:3

8. OTHERS:
  - DISREGARD FOR OTHERS John 13:34
  - DISREGARD FOR GOD'S SOVEREIGNTY Matthew 6:9-10
  - UNSURRENDERED WILL/ REBELLION John 15:7, Hebrews 12:15
  - LUST Matthew 5:28
  - COMPLAINING Ephesians 4:32
  - IMPATIENCE WITH OTHERS Ephesians 4:26, 31
  - STRIFE Colossians 3:9
  - PRAYERLESSNESS James 1
  - BITTERNESS James 1:6
  - NOT THANKFUL / GRATEFUL Philippians 4:4-8
  - LYING I Corinthians 10:10
  - UNRESOLVED CONFLICTS MATTHEW 5:23

IS JESUS YOUR 1st LOVE ? (IDOLS IN TODAY'S WORLD)

Most Christians believe that they do not have any idols in their life. To most people idols are some type of religious or pagan statue or carving. That is what idols were in the Old Testament of the Bible.

Would it surprise you to find out that many of us Christians have idols in our life ? These days idols are not what most people think they are.

God's Word is very clear about how He feels about our idols. God's view of Idols:

Deuteronomy 5:7 - God zealously loves us with all His being & wants us to love Him this same way

"I will pronounce my judgements on my people because of their wickedness in forsaking me, in burning incense to other gods and in worshipping what their hands have made. ... I remember the devotion of your youth, how as a bride you loved me and followed me through the desert... Has a nation ever changed its gods ? (Yet they are not gods at all.) But my people have exchanged my Glory for worthless idols. ... My people have committed two sins: they have forsaken me, the spring of living water, and have dug their own cisterns, broken cisterns that cannot hold water. ... Have you not brought this on yourselves by forsaking the Lord your God when he led you in the way ? ... Your wickedness will punish you; your backsliding will rebuke you. Consider then and realize how evil and bitter it is for you when you forsake the Lord your God and have no awe of me. ... They have turned their backs to me and not their faces; yet when they are in trouble they say, 'Come and save us !' Where then are the gods you made for yourselves ? Let them come if they can save you when you are in trouble ! ... But you have lived as a prostitute with many lovers – would you now return to me ? ... their immorality mattered so little to them, they defiled the land and committed adultery with stone and wood (idols). ... Only acknowledge your guilt- you have rebelled against the Lord your God, you have scattered your favors to foreign gods under every spreading tree and have not obeyed me; Return, faithless people, declares the Lord, for I am your husband. ... How gladly would I treat you like sons and give you a desirable land, the most beautiful inheritance of any nation. I thought you would call me Father, and not turn away from following me. But like a woman unfaithful to her husband, so you have been unfaithful to me." (excerpts from Jeremiah 1:16 to 3:20)

God views our idols as acts of ***adultery*** in our relationship with Him

"Do not love the world or anything in the world. If anyone loves the world, the love of the Father is not in him. For everything in the world – the cravings of sinful man, the lust of his eyes and the boasting of what he has and does – comes not from the Father but from the world." – I John 2:15-16

Examples Of Today's Idols

- Religion
- Tradition
- Pleasure
- Career
- Success
- Accomplishment
- Money or Material Things
- Status
- Power or Influence
- Position
- Our own goals and will
- Control
- Our own ideas
- Our own opinions
- Self – living to please self instead of pleasing God

2 Corinthians 5:9, 14-15 - "Therefore we also have as our ambition, whether at home or absent, to be pleasing to Him… For the love of Christ controls us, having concluded this, that one died for all, therefore all died; and He died for all, so that they who live might no longer live for themselves, but for Him who died and rose again on their behalf."

It's not wrong to have these things. It becomes wrong when we begin to love these things and turn to them to satisfy and fulfill ourselves, and when we love these things or desire these things more than we love and desire God.

Here are some questions to ask yourself to see if you may have some idols in your life. Spend time with God and ask Him to search your heart as you review the following questions:

What do you treasure and value and desire most ?

- Matthew 6:21

- God wants to be your treasure, since He treasures you most

What do you seek after or pursue most ?

- Proverbs 21:21

- Matthew 6:33 - "Seek **first** God's kingdom and righteousness…"

- God wants you to pursue and seek Him, and be your **first love**

What takes most of your time & focus & energy ?

- Colossians 3:1-5

- God wants you to set your heart and mind on Him and His kingdom

What do you put your trust in ?

- Proverbs 3:5-6

- God wants you to trust in Him with all your heart

What do you think will satisfy and fulfill you ?

- Isaiah 55:1-3

- Psalm 63:1-5

- Psalm 81

- John 10:10

- God wants to give you abundant life & fully fill and satisfy your heart & soul

What are some things you are not willing to let go of ?

- Philippians 3:7-9

- you need to be willing to love and follow Jesus, whatever the cost

Why do you do the things you do ?

- I Chronicles 28:9

- Matthew 22:37-40

- Your motives should be love for God and love for others

"God looks down from heaven on the sons of men to see if there are any who understand, any who seek God." – Psalm 53:2

"Yet you have not called upon me… you have not wearied yourselves for me." – Isaiah 43:22

"All of us have become like one who is unclean, and all our righteous acts are like filthy rags; we all shrivel up like a leaf, and like the wind our sins sweep us away. No one calls on your name or strives to lay hold of you." -Isaiah 64:6-7

"I will sprinkle clean water on you, and you will be clean; I will cleanse you from your impurities and from all your idols. I will give you a new heart and put a new spirit in you; I will remove from you your heart of stone and give you a heart of flesh. And I will put my Spirit in you and move you to follow my decrees and be careful to keep my laws…You will be my people, and I will be your God." – Ezekiel 36:25-28

" I will give them a heart to know Me, that I am the Lord. They will be My people and I will be their God, for they will return to Me with all their heart." – Jeremiah 24:7

"If my people, who are called by My name, will humble themselves, and pray and seek My face and turn from their wicked ways, then will I hear from heaven and will forgive their sin and will heal their land. Now my eyes will be open and my ears attentive to the prayers offered in this place." – 2 Chronicles 7:14

" Even now, declares the Lord, return to me with all your heart, with fasting and weeping and mourning. Rend your heart and not your garments. Return to the Lord your God, for he is gracious and compassionate, slow to anger and abounding in love, and he relents from sending calamity." – Joel 2:12-13

Jesus wants to be your **First Love**, since you are His first love

PURE HEART: PURE LOVE & DEVOTION & PASSION FOR GOD

SUPERNATURAL,　　　　　　　　NATURAL, CARNAL
SPIRITUAL (JESUS)　　　　　　　　　(US)

GOD & OTHERS	GOD & OTHERS | SELF

Fully Surrendered (**Hebrews 5:7**)	Rebellious (**Is. 1:19-20, Rom. 8:5-8**)
Fully Devoted to God (**John 4:34, 5:30**)	Denies Jesus (**John 13:36-38**)
	Self-centered, Selfish (**Jer. 17:9-14, Gal. 5:19-21**)
Fully Obedient (**Heb. 5:8, Luke 22:42**)	Disobedient (**Rom. 7:18-8:8**)
Fully Dependant on God (**John 5:19,30**)	Self-dependent (**John 15:5, 2 Cor. 3:4-5**)
Love for God, Others (**I John 3:16, 4:16**)	Loves Self, World,...(**Gal. 5:20, I John 2:15-17**)

EXAMPLES OF PURE LOVE / DEVOTION / PASSION FOR GOD
Mary — **Mark 14:3-9** "she has done a beautiful thing to Me."
David — **Psalm 16:8-11** ; **Psalm 63:3** ; **Psalm 86:11** ; **Acts 13:22**
Joseph — **Genesis 39:6-9**
Paul — **Philippians 3:7-11**; **2 Corinthians 5:9, 14**; **Galatians 2:20**
Paul's source of grace & power, faith, and love & devotion for God: **I Timothy 1:12-14**

"Give me an undivided heart." - **Psalm 86:11**
"Create in me a pure heart & renew a steadfast spirit in me." - **Psalm 51:10**
"Turn my heart toward your statutes and not toward selfish gain. Turn my eyes from worthless things (idols); preserve my life according to your word." - **Psalm 119:36-37**

"Because of the increase of wickedness, the love of most will grow cold" (**Matt. 24:12**)- This waning of love refers to the dying out of the fire of a holy passion for the Lord Himself and for those for whom He gave His life, the loss of holy enthusiasm in His service and devotion. It refers not to that fleshly enthusiasm in His service and devotion that shouts & rejoices when the crowd is coming, or works zealously when the brass band is playing and the grandstand is filled with admirers. No! No! It is that enthusiasm that works with a quiet, untiring, unassuming earnestness & steadiness when it must plod on alone unheard and unnoticed except by the Lord- that enthusiasm that is born not of outward encouragement, nor the applause of men, nor by what men call success, nor by the unholy desire for praise, but that which is born of an inward urge implanted by the Holy Spirit, the overflow of the **passion** of Christ. The waning of this love, said Jesus, will be one of the earmarks of the end times.
- E.S. Gerig

WEEK 5 STUDY REVIEW (Pages 56-63)

q MARK T FOR TRUE AND F FOR FALSE (See Page 56, 63):
___ We don't need God to search our hearts. ___ We fully understand what is in our hearts.
___ Our motives are always pure & unselfish. ___ It takes a pure heart to see and know God.
___ Part of having a pure heart is to have pure love & devotion & passion for God.
___ We naturally love God with a pure heart, and love Him more than anything, including self.
___ We need God to cleanse us and change us, so that we can love Him with a pure heart
___ True love for God ("agape" love) will involve submission, commitment, and sacrifice.

q READ **PSALM 51:4** ; WE NEED TO REALIZE THAT WHEN WE SIN, WE AREN'T SINNING AGAINST A SET OF RULES, BUT PERSONALLY AGAINST GOD.

q TRUE SORROW FOR YOUR SIN AGAINST GOD & TRUE CONFESSION MEANS:
___ You are sorry -- for getting caught and now having to pay the price for it.
___ It's ok to keep sinning the same ways over & over , just as long as you keep confessing.
___ True sorrow for personally hurting & offending God leads you to repent/ turn/ change.

q PRAYERFULLY REVIEW PAGES 59-62 AND ASK GOD TO REVEAL ANY HIDDEN SINS OR IDOLS IN YOUR HEART & LIFE, THEN CONFESS/ RECONNECT WITH HIM.

q REVIEW JOHN 4:34, LUKE 22:42, JOHN 5:19,30 & 14:31; CHOOSE THE STATEMENTS THAT ARE TRUE:
___ Jesus lived His earthly life trying to fulfill His own desires and plans and goals and dreams.
___ Jesus' main motivation was to do His Father's will.
___ Jesus did not struggle at all and did not need to pray for God's help in order to obey God concerning dying on the cross. (see Luke 22:39-46)
___ Even though Jesus struggled & agonized to the point of sweating blood & water, He prayed and received the strength and power to obey His Father's will to die on the cross.
___ Jesus obeyed and followed God's will because He loved God, His Father.

q READ JOHN 13:36-38 (Page 63); PETER SINCERELY TOLD JESUS THAT HE WOULD FOLLOW HIM ANYWHERE, BUT HE ENDED UP DENYING JESUS. LATER, PETER GAVE HIS LIFE FOR JESUS, AND DIED UPSIDE DOWN ON A CROSS. MARK THE STATEMENTS THAT ARE TRUE:
___ Sincerely trying your best (in your ability, strength,...) will be good enough for following God
___ We naturally will love and follow God, no matter what He leads us to do.
___ We naturally want to follow our will, and our plans & desires,...
___ It was the "filling" of the Holy Spirit in Peter (Acts 1:8) that made the big difference.
___ Our natural love & devotion for God will always end up falling short of full surrender to God

q PAUL WAS ONE OF THE MOST PASSIONATE SERVANTS OF JESUS, AND GOD USED HIM IN POWERFUL WAYS; READ **PHIL. 3:7-11, 2 COR. 5:9,14-15**, AND **I TIMOTHY 1:12-14**; WHICH IS TRUE ?:
___ Paul was a strong person, and had a natural passion & love & devotion for God and for Jesus
___ Paul got his strength & power (grace) and faith and love/devotion/passion for God from Jesus, via His Holy Spirit. (see I Timothy 1:12-14)

Get face to face with God and prayerfully review this week's material. Ask God to show you how you can be closer to Him and more one with Him

IT'S THE RELATIONSHIP !!!

WORSHIP & PRAISE GOD (ADORE HIM):
- GLORIFY HIM - FOCUS - SOFT HEART (Listening; Willing; Obedient)
(Isaiah 1:19,20; I Sam. 15:22,23; Psalm 37:4 ;...)

HEAR FROM GOD , READ GOD'S WORD (GOD PERSONALLY SPEAKS TO YOU)
- DON'T JUST QUICKLY READ GOD'S WORD
- **OBSERVE & HEAR** ALL YOU POSSIBLY CAN, **INTERPRET, APPLY**

MEDITATE ON GOD , HIS WORKS, AND ON HIS WORD: (Joshua 1:8)
- WHAT ARE YOU SAYING TO ME GOD ?
- HOW DOES MY CIRCUMSTANCES, WHAT GODLY PEOPLE ARE SAYING, AND WHAT I SENSE IN PRAYER CONFIRM THIS ?
- HOW CAN I APPLY / DO THIS IN MY LIFE ? (James 1:22-25) (Luke 11:28)

PRAYER - COMMUNICATE, RESPOND, INTERACT & FELLOWSHIP WITH GOD:
- COMMUNICATE INTIMATELY WITH GOD
- FIND OUT WHAT HE IS TRYING TO SAY TO YOU OR TEACH YOU
- ASK GOD TO HELP YOU TO YIELD TO HIM & OBEY & FOLLOW HIM

JOHN 15: 13,14
I JOHN 5:3
REV. 2:1-4
PROOF OF LOVE FOR GOD

SUBMIT & OBEY

GRACE

CONFESS & RECONNECT TO GOD
(SIN & DISOBEDIENCE IS PERSONALLY AGAINST GOD)(PSALM 51:4 ; I JOHN 1:9)

1. GOD WILL ENHANCE YOUR RELATIONSHIP WITH HIM (John 14:21)
2. GOD WILL SHOW HIMSELF TO YOU (Matt. 5: 8, 16:15-17 ; John 14:21)
3. GOD IS FREE TO FILL YOU WITH HIS SPIRIT (Ephesians 5:18) AND LIVE & WORK IN & THROUGH YOU (John 14:10-14; 15:5-17; Galatians 2:20)

AS YOU SUBMIT TO GOD AND ALLOW HIM TO WORK IN YOU, HE WILL CHANGE YOU AND YOUR CHARACTER TO BE MORE LIKE JESUS, AND TO BE CLOSER TO HIM, AND ONE WITH HIM & HIS WAYS & PLANS & PURPOSES

GOD WANTS TO TRANSFORM YOU & MOLD AND SHAPE YOU
   * INTIMATE & ONE WITH GOD (see John 15 & John 17)
   * YOU GO FROM DOING TO BEING (be loving, be His witness,...)
   * GOD INCREASES & YOU DECREASE (John 3:30)
   * GOD EXPANDS YOUR LIFE & SERVICE FOR HIM (Prayer of Jabez)
   * ABUNDANT & FULL LIFE (John 10:10) (Matthew 16:25)
   * YOU ARE RIGHTEOUS (James 5:16b)
   * YOU ARE A TRUE DISCIPLE (Luke 9:23)
   * YOU ARE MORE & MORE LIKE CHRIST (Romans 8:29, 2 Corinthians 3:18)

GOD'S ULTIMATE GOAL FOR YOU:
TO BE LIKE JESUS – A PERSON OF HONOR & GLORY

God wants you to be the very best person you can be, and He wants to share His glory with you and have you become more and more like His Son Jesus ... full of His love, joy, peace, patience, kindness, goodness, faithfulness, gentleness, self control, power, grace, faith,...

- Romans 12:1,2 - "... offer your bodies as living sacrifices, holy and pleasing to God - this is your spiritual act of worship. Do not conform any longer to the pattern of this world, but be **transformed** ("metamorphosis") by the renewing of your mind."

- Romans 8:17,18 - "Now if we are children, then we are heirs - heirs of God and co-heirs with Christ, if indeed we share in his sufferings in order that we may also **share in His glory**. I consider that our present sufferings are not worth comparing with the **glory** that will be revealed in us."

- Romans 8:28,29 - "And we know that in all things God works for the good of those who love Him (Seek Him / Trust Him / Submit to Him / Obey & Follow Him)... For those God foreknew he also predestined (planned from the beginning) to be **conformed** (transformed) **to the likeness of His Son**..."

- 2 Corinthians 3:18 - "And we, who with unveiled faces all reflect the Lord's **glory**, are being **transformed into His likeness** with ever-increasing **glory** ("glory to glory"), which comes from the Lord, who is the Spirit."

- Luke 9:29,30 - "As he (Jesus) was praying, the appearance of his face changed, and his clothes became as bright as a flash of lightning. Two men, Moses and Elijah, appeared in **glorious splendor**, talking with Jesus."

- Matthew 13:43 - "Then the righteous will **shine** like the sun in the kingdom of their Father."

- Daniel 12:3 - "Those who are wise will **shine** like the brightness of the heavens, and those who lead many to righteousness, like the stars forever and ever."

- Philippians 3:8-14 - "... I consider everything a loss compared to the surpassing greatness of knowing Christ Jesus my Lord, for whose sake I have lost all things. I consider them rubbish that I may gain Christ ... I want to know Christ and the power of His resurrection and the fellowship of sharing in His sufferings, becoming like Him in His death,... forgetting what is behind and straining toward what is ahead, I press on toward the goal to win the prize for which God has called me heavenward in Christ Jesus."

(Teleos - Perfect, Complete, Mature ; Phil. 3:12, James 1:4, Col. 4:12, Eph. 4:11-13,...)

"To fulfill God's perfect design for you requires your total surrender - complete abandonment of yourself to Him." - Oswald Chambers

WHAT DOES IT MEAN TO BE A PERSON OF GLORY ?

Webster's Dictionary: "Distinguished Praise and Honor"

WHAT IS GOD'S GLORY ? IT'S HIS GLORIOUS CHARACTER
- Exodus 33:18-19- "Then Moses said, now show me your glory. And the Lord said, I will cause all my **goodness** to pass in front of you,... I will have **mercy**...I will have **compassion**..."

- Exodus 34:6-7 - " And he passed in front of Moses, proclaiming "The Lord, the Lord, the **compassionate** and **gracious** God, **slow to anger**, **abounding in love**, and **faithfulness**, maintaining **love** to thousands, and **forgiving** wickedness, rebellion and sin. Yet he does not leave the guilty unpunished..." (**just** and **holy**)

- Galatians 5:22,23 - "But the fruit of the Spirit is **love, joy, peace, patience, kindness, goodness, faithfulness, gentleness, self-control**."

- Revelation 1:12-18 - "...His face was like the sun shining in all it's brilliance..."

- Isaiah 6:1-3; Rev. 4:8 - "**Holy, holy, holy** is the Lord Almighty" (morally perfect & pure)

WE WILL HAVE GOD'S GLORY (HIS LOVE, GOODNESS,...) FOREVER IN HEAVEN, TO THE DEGREE WE LIVE FOR CHRIST & GROW LIKE CHRIST HERE ON EARTH:

- 2 Corinthians 4:10, 17-18 - "We always carry around in our body the death of Christ, so that the life of Jesus may also be revealed in our body." v.17,18 - "For our light and momentary troubles are achieving for us an **eternal glory** that far outweighs them all. So we fix our eyes not on what is seen, but on what is unseen. For what is seen in temporary, but what is unseen is eternal."

- 2 Corinthians 5:9,10 - "So we make it our goal to please Him, whether we are at home in the body or away from it. For we must all appear before the judgment seat of Christ, that each one may receive what is due him for the things done while in the body, whether good or bad."

- Hebrews 11:6 - "And without faith it is impossible to please God, because anyone who comes to Him must believe that He exists and that He **rewards** those who **earnestly seek** Him."
- also read **John 12:23-26** , **Luke 9:23-25** , **Philippians 2:5-11**

- I Peter 5:1-4 - "I appeal as a fellow elder, a witness of Christ's sufferings and one who also will **share in the glory** to be revealed... be eager to serve... And when the Chief Shepherd appears, you will receive the **crown of glory** that will never fade away."

(crown- Greek stephanos: a royal exalted rank; eternal blessedness which will be given as a prize to the **genuine servants** of Christ; an ornament of honor) (Rev. 4:4,10; 2 Tim. 4:7-8)

"He is no fool who loses what he cannot keep, to gain what he cannot lose."   - Jim Elliott

GOD'S CALL FOR YOUR LIFE

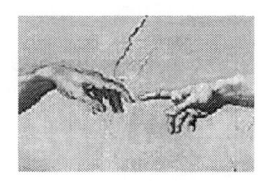

What is God's call for your life ? That is the question many Christians wonder about and seek an answer to. Is it for full time ministry, or to be a missionary, or to be a lay person, or ...? God's word offers some insight into His calling and His plans & will for His people.

You need to prayerfully seek God and ask Him to help you to discern His special plan and calling for your life, and ask Him to give you the faith and courage to follow, wherever He leads you. You will be happiest and full of joy when you are in the middle of God's will and plan.

SOME GUIDELINES FROM GOD'S WORD:

1. GOD'S CALL FIRST IS TO A RESTORED RELATIONSHIP AND THEN TO CLOSE FELLOWSHIP WITH HIM:

Only by accepting and receiving Jesus Christ as your Lord and Savior will you ever be reconciled to God and be able to have a personal relationship with Him.

- "I (Jesus) am the way, the truth, and the life. No one comes to the Father except through me."- John 14:6
- " to all who received Jesus, to those who believed in his name, he gave the right to become children of God." – John 1:12

Eternal life and being a Christian is not just about accepting Jesus as your Lord & Savior, then waiting around to go to heaven where you will live forever. It is about a relationship with God, and getting to know Him , and serving Him and obeying Him because you love Him.

- "Now this is eternal life: that they may know you the only true God and Jesus Christ, whom you have sent" – John 17:3
- " I have called you friends." – John 15:15
- " You are my friends if you do what I command." – John 15:14

- "God's call is for you to be His loyal friend, for whatever purpose He has for your life." – Oswald Chambers "My Utmost For His Highest"

- "God, who has called you into fellowship ("koinania") with His Son Jesus Christ our Lord, is faithful." – I Corinthians 1:9

"koinania" fellowship- the closest possible intimate fellowship with God, unity and oneness with God, and also a partnership with God in His kingdom work and mission.

2. GOD HAS A SPECIAL & UNIQUE PURPOSE AND PLAN FOR YOUR LIFE:

- " For I know the plans I have for you, declares the Lord, plans to prosper you and not to harm you, plans to give you hope and a future." – Jeremiah 29:11

Jeremiah 29:11 tells us that God has special plans for our lives, plans to bless us and prosper us; The next two verses spell out the necessary conditions for us to receive the benefit of His plans

- "Then when you call upon Me and come and pray to Me, I will hear you. When you search for Me, You will find Me; if you seek Me with all your heart"– Jeremiah 29:12-13

- " God will instruct him in the way chosen for him." – Psalm 25:12

- " You are a chosen people, a royal priesthood, a holy nation, a people belonging to God, that you may declare the praises of Him who called you out of darkness into His wonderful light." – I Peter 2:9

- " For we are God's workmanship ("valuable masterpiece"), created in Christ Jesus to do good works, which God prepared in advance for us to do." – Ephesians 2:10

3. GOD PLACES A DESIRE AND A PASSION IN OUR HEARTS TO DO THE THINGS HE CALLS US TO DO:

- " For it is God who works in you to will and to act according to His good purpose." – Philippians 2:13

- You will have a love & joy & passion for doing the things God has created you for & calls you to do

4. GOD GIVES SPIRITUAL GIFTS TO EQUIP YOU FOR YOUR CALLING:

- God gives each Christian spiritual gifts through the Holy Spirit.
- Spiritual gifts are for the building up and edifying of the body of Christ, His church
- See pages for the list of Spiritual Gifts

5. GOD'S PRESENCE & POWER WILL ALWAYS BE WITH YOU WHEN HE CALLS YOU:

- "Set apart for me Barnabas & Saul for the work to which I have called them."– Acts 13:2

The Greek word for called means that God "*called them unto Himself*"... first to a love relationship with God, and next to where God's *presence* and *power* would be at work.

We only need to respond in faith and obedience, and God will provide the power and whatever else is needed to get the job done.

Moses being called to help lead God's people out of Egypt is another good example of God's call and how God provided everything (see Exodus 3 & 4)

6. THERE ARE SOME THINGS THAT GOD CALLS ALL CHRISTIANS TO DO:

- "Come follow Me, and I will make you fishers of men." – Matthew 4:19
- "Then Jesus came to them and said "All authority in heaven and on earth have been given to me. Therefore, go and make disciples of all nations, baptizing them in the name of the Father and of the Son and of the Holy Spirit, and teaching them to obey everything I have commanded you." – Matthew 28:18-20

You are not ***truly following Jesus*** unless you are being a fisher of men and an active witness for Jesus Christ, telling the lost about Him and sharing His plan of salvation with them. He also wants you and other believers the church to help & teach others to become fully devoted and passionate disciples (learners and followers) of Jesus Christ, so they will be fruitful witnesses and servants of His.

In Acts 8:1 there was a great persecution that came against the church, and the apostles (leaders & pastors) stayed in Jerusalem and the regular people of the church were scattered to other places (Judea and Samaria).

Acts 8:4 shows that "**all** of those that were scattered preached the word (gospel) of the Lord Jesus wherever they went... All of the people in the church, not just the pastors and leaders, went out and shared the Gospel with as many people they could, in every place they went.

The job and task of sharing Christ and the Gospel with others is not just the job of the pastors and church leaders. Jesus commanded all believers, all followers/disciples of His to do it.

FINDING GOD'S WILL & VISION FOR YOUR LIFE & MINISTRY

Someone once asked Dr. Bill Bright , founder of Campus Crusade For Christ, how did you know what God was calling you to do with your life ? I keep waiting to find my purpose, but feel so lost. Dr. Bright said "the most important way to know God's will is to **totally surrender** to the Lordship of Christ. Ask Him to guide your steps. You are in God's will if you are surrendered to Him. The God who created everything guides our steps. All He wants is surrender and he'll tell us what he wants us to do. Don't give much thought to what you will do in the future ... Surrender to Him now and he will guide you in the rest. I live by Philippians 2:13 "for it is God who works in you both to will and to act according to His good purpose." So as I walk in the Spirit I can know that God will guide my steps. For example, in 1951 my wife and I decided we wanted to be total servants to Jesus. We wrote out a contract and fully surrendered everything we owned or would own to Jesus. Approximately 24 hours later God gave me the vision we called Campus Crusade For Christ. I'm sure if there had been no surrender and contract with God there would have been no vision. You can know God's will by **full surrender to Christ**, and by allowing the Holy Spirit to control you."

"To fulfill God's perfect design for you requires your **total surrender** - complete abandonment of yourself to Him." - Oswald Chambers

SPIRITUAL GIFTS

Administration: the gift that enables a believer to formulate, direct, and carry out plans necessary to fulfill a purpose.

- I Corinthians 12:28
- Acts 14:23

Discernment: the Holy Spirit given ability to distinguish whether someone or something is of God or not of God.

- John 16:6-15
- Romans 9:1
- I Corinthians 2:9-16, 12:10

Exhortation: The Holy Spirit produced ability to challenge, strengthen, encourage, and comfort believers.

- John 14:1
- 2 Timothy 1:16-18
- 3 John 5-8

Faith: the Holy Spirit given ability to trust God where others will not, and to see something that God wants done and sustain unwavering confidence that God will do it regardless of seemingly insurmountable obstacles.

- Genesis 12:1-4a
- Mark 5:25-34
- 1 Thessalonians 1:8-10

Giving: the gift that enables a believer to recognize God's blessings and to respond to those blessings by generously and sacrificially giving of one's resources (time, talent, and treasure).

- Luke 21:1-4

- Romans 12:8
- 2 Corinthians 9:6-15

Knowledge: the gift that drives a person to learn, analyze and uncover new insights with regard to the Bible and faith.

- 1 Corinthians 12:8
- 1 Corinthians 14:6
- Romans 12:2

Leadership: the gift that gives a believer the confidence to step forward, give direction and provide motivation to fulfill a dream or complete a task.

- Romans 12:8
- John 21:15-17
- 2 Timothy 4:1-5

Mercy: the Holy Spirit given ability to see those who are in misery, have pity on them, and promptly & cheerfully seek to relieve them of their need.

- Matthew 25:34-36
- Luke 7:12-15, 10:30-37
- Romans 12:8

Prophecy: an ability given by God's Holy Spirit to proclaim God's truth publicly and to apply it practically, with a view to correction and edification.

- Romans 12:6
- 1 Corinthians 12:10, 14:1,3

Service/ Helps: the gift that enables a believer to work gladly behind the scenes in order that God's work is fulfilled.

- Luke 23:50-54
- Romans 12:7, 16:1-16
- Philippians 2:19-23

Teaching: the Holy Spirit produced ability to effectively explain God's word and apply it.

- Matthew 5:1-12
- Acts 18:24-48
- Romans 12:7
- 1 Corinthians 12:28

Wisdom: skilled in the application of Biblical truth; is able to take God's Word and apply it to everyday situations.

- I Corinthians 2:6-13
- James 3:13-18
- 2 Chronicles 1:7-11

WEEK 6 STUDY REVIEW (Pages 66-75)

q REVIEW PAGE 66; CHOOSE THE STATEMENTS THAT ARE TRUE & CORRECT:
___ The key to a right and intimate relationship with God is knowing the right formula of things to do (praise + read Bible + meditate + pray = Intimacy With God).
___ It's not just what you do, but also how you do them and why you do them (what is in your heart).
___ The proof of love for God is you trust and love Him enough to submit yourself and your life into His hands and follow & obey what He tells you or leads you to do (I John 5:3,..)
___ Jesus' idea of prayer and love for God is: "not my will, but your will be done."

q TRUE OR FALSE: YOU CAN OBEY AND FOLLOW JESUS CONSISTENTLY WITHOUT FULLY SUBMITTING YOURSELF AND YOUR LIFE TO HIM.

q READ **JOHN 14:15-23** ; MARK T FOR TRUE OR F FOR FALSE:
___ You can have a close relationship with God without having to obey and follow God
___ Submitting yourself, obeying, and following Jesus and His ways and commands will lead you to a closer relationship with Him.
___ Submitting, obeying, and following Jesus will also lead to you being able to see Him and know Him more and more ("... I too will love him and show myself to him.")
___ Another result of submitting, obeying, and following Jesus: He will be able to fill you more and more with His life (abundant life), and He will live & work in and through you.

q WHICH OF THESE ARE SOME OF GOD'S PLANS AND GOALS FOR YOU:
___ God wants you to ascend up the "church ladder" of status and position.
___ God wants to take you from doing kind acts, loving acts, ... to being a kind person, being a loving person, being a patient person, being a forgiving person,...
___ God wants you to be intimate with Him and one with Him and His will and ways.
___ God wants you to have full and abundant life (His life flowing in and through you)
___ God wants to make you an instrument of His to reach a lost world (Matt. 4:19)
___ God wants to you to become a famous Christian and write books and get on tv.
___ God's ultimate goal for you is to become more and more like Jesus.

q READ 2 CORINTHIANS 12:2-4 & THEN REVIEW PAGE 66 & 67; CHOOSE THE CORRECT STATEMENTS:

___ When Paul wrote about being "transformed" and "sharing in Jesus' glory" and about eternity in heaven (Rom. 12:1-2; Rom. 8:17-18, 28-29 ; 2 Cor. 3:18,...) he was writing about things that he thought or speculated might possibly happen.

___ Paul wrote about these things authoritatively, because God revealed them to Him and he was allowed to see heaven (paradise) and see God's ultimate goal for His children (see **1 Cor. 2:6-10** and **2 Cor. 12:2-4**)

___ Paul saw and understood that knowing Jesus through an intimate love relationship, knowing His life & love & power flowing through Him, and becoming like Jesus was the ultimate "**prize**" (Phil. 3:14), and he totally abandoned himself to Jesus and passionately served Him.

___ Paul clearly understood the truth that our life here will determine who we will be for eternity, and the more like Jesus we become here in this life will determine how much of God's glory we will share and have forever in God's eternal kingdom.

**Get face to face with God and prayerfully review this week's material.
Ask God to show youhow you can be closer to Him and more one with Him**

PURSUING INTIMACY WITH GOD II

www.intimacywithgod.com

God's Greatest Desire

What is God's greatest desire for you ? God sees you as a precious treasure, and He longs to have close fellowship with you. More than anything He wants you to have an intimate love relationship and friendship with Him. God longs for you to spend time with Him daily and intimately communicate with Him, to hear His voice, to enjoy fellowship with Him, to trust and follow Him, and to give your life meaning and purpose.

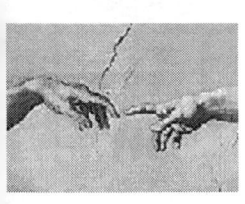

Do you desire a deeper and closer relationship and friendship with God ? Is your desire to know Him and to please Him growing ? Do you want to know God in real & personal ways, rather than just knowing about Him ? Do you know that hearing God's voice is by far the most important part of your prayer/fellowship time with God ? Because you are precious to Him and He greatly loves you, God wants to be your first love and have first place in your life.

If you answered yes to any of these questions, then this in-depth Bible study is for you. Although it may mean making changes in your life and in your daily schedule, you can have the fullest and closest possible fellowship and partnership with God throughout the rest of your life. Any Christian can have this wonderful intimacy with God, and experience the abundant and full and meaningful life that God designed you to have. Always remember that God wants intimacy with you and He wants you to have the abundant life He promises more than you want it. As you seek Him and desire with all of your heart to have an intimate fellowship with God, He will always be there to help you every step of the way.

Pursuing Intimacy With God II is a 6 week study that carefully examines God's Word to help you to learn to hear God's voice; to see what it takes to have a powerful prayer life like Jesus did; to help you to pray Biblically and effectively for the lost people you know, and also for your pastor & staff, your church, and your country; to see that God wants to bless you and take of you and your family's needs; to experience Jesus setting you free in all areas of your life; to know Jesus as your source of abundant life and joy and peace and...; to learn that faith is absolutely vital to intimacy with God, and how to get the strong faith that pleases Him; to encourage you and help you when God makes you wait for Him; to understand God's spiritual goals for you and the tools that He uses you to get you to be all that He wants you to be; to give you some good practical tips for making the most of your prayer & fellowship time with god; and to learn what true and total commitment and surrender to Jesus means.

It is our prayer that, through the power and grace of the Holy Spirit, God will greatly bless you in your fellowship and walk with Him through this study, and that He will reveal His glory and beauty to you, and that He will also reveal the wonderful and amazing plans that He has for you. God bless you as you seek intimacy with Him.

"I keep asking that the God of our Lord Jesus Christ, the glorious Father, may give you the Spirit of wisdom and revelation, so that you may know him better." (Ephesians 1:17)

PURSUING INTIMACY WITH GOD

Welcome to the Pursuing Intimacy With God Bible study. This Bible study and ministry is dedicated to helping you to pursue and ultimately receive the fullest and most intimate fellowship and oneness and partnership with Jesus Christ.

There is one very critical issue that needs to be settled before you can ever begin to deepen your relationship and fellowship with God ... do you have a reconciled personal relationship with God ? What are the requirements and details of Salvation & Gospel of Jesus Christ

There are many people these days that believe that God does not exist. There are many others that believe that God is some far away, impersonal spirit that takes pleasure in punishing people and making their life difficult. Sometimes if a person has had a bad experience with their own father, or had a father that abandoned them, they will have a hard time seeing God for who He really is. And it will then be difficult to personally know God.

The Bible tells us that God is not some far away impersonal spirit. God can seem that way to some people, and it is more challenging to many because God is not visible to us. Acts 17:27 says "that they would seek God, if perhaps they might grope for Him and find Him, though He is not far from each one of us." The Bible promises us in many verses that if we will seek to personally know God, then we will find Him and ultimately know Him.

God is a loving and caring personal love-relationship oriented father. He loves us and He very much desires to have a restored relationship with us. "God desires all men to be saved and to come to the knowledge of the truth." - I Timothy 2:4. God wants everyone to be saved... to first have a restored relationship with Him, then close fellowship with Him, and ultimately eternal life with Him in heaven when our life here is done.

The first important thing in order to begin to know God for who He really is, and have close fellowship with Him and personally know God: You have to have a restored or reconciled relationship with God. God's Word the Bible clearly shows that we all have a broken relationship with God because of our sins, and that we need to have this taken care of. Many people try to solve this problem of sin and separation from God and a broken relationship with Him themselves. People try many things to try to reach out to God and personally know Him... they try Religion, or Philosophy, or Church, or doing good things, or giving money to charity...

Also, we are all created with a built in need to personally know God and have a restored relationship and fellowship with Him. When this need is not met, then we will have a void in our life. Many people do not know what it is, but they will know that something is missing in their life or that something is not right. People will try all types of things to try to fill this void in their life... Relationships with people, Sex, Drugs, Alcohol, Pleasure, Recreation, Money, Career,...

Salvation & The Gospel of Jesus Christ (A Restored Relationship With God):

Step 1: God loves you and wants you to experience peace and life – abundant and eternal life:

- "We have peace with God through our Lord Jesus Christ." – Romans 5:1
- "For God so loved the world that he gave his one and only Son, that whoever believes in him shall not perish but have everlasting life." – John 3:16

- God loves you so much that He sent His only Son Jesus to suffer and then die a very painful death on a cross, to make it possible for us to have a restored relationship with Him.
- "I have come that they may have life, and that they may have it more abundantly." – John 10:10

Step 2: The Problem – Our Sin & Separation From God:
- "For all have sinned and fall short of the glory of God." – Romans 3:23
- "For the wages of sin is death (eternal separation from God), but the gift of God is eternal life in Christ Jesus our Lord." – Romans 6:23
- "But your iniquities have separated you from your God; your sins have hidden his face from you, so that he will not hear." – Isaiah 59:2
- Our sins are personally against God, and cause us to have a broken relationship with Him, and to be separated from Him.
- Sin is not just breaking some religious rule or law. Sin is personally against God… "Against You, You only, I have sinned And done what is evil in Your sight, So that You are justified when You speak And blameless when You judge." - Psalm 51:4 Our Attempts To Reach God:
- people have tried in many ways to bridge this gap and separation between themselves and God … good works, religion, philosophy, morality,… and none work … except One
- "There is a way that seems right to a man, but in the end it leads to death." – Proverbs 14:12
- Jesus said "I am the way, the truth, and the life. No one may come to the Father except through me." – John 14:6

Step 3: God's Solution To Our Problem – Salvation & Gospel of Jesus Christ And The Cross:
- "For there is one God and one mediator between God and men, the man Jesus Christ." – I Timothy 2:5
- "For Christ died for sins once for all, the righteous for the unrighteous, to bring you to God." – I Peter 3:18
- "But God demonstrates his own love for us in this: While we were still sinners, Christ died for us." – Romans 5:8
- Jesus is God's answer and solution to our problem of sin, eternal separation from God, and eternal punishment for our sins.
- "For God so loved the world that he gave his one and only Son, that whoever believes in him shall not perish but have everlasting life." – John 3:16
- Jesus said "I am the way, the truth, and the life. No one may come to the Father *except through me.*" – John 14:6

Step 4: Our Response: Repent, Put Your Faith in Jesus, and Receive Christ As Your Lord & Savior:
- you must trust Jesus Christ as your Lord and Savior and receive Him by faith and personal invitation:
- "Here I am! I stand at the door and knock. If anyone hears my voice and opens the door, I will come in and eat with him, and he with me." – Revelation 3:20
- "That if you confess with your mouth "Jesus is Lord", and believe in your heart that God raised him from the dead, you will be saved." – Romans 10:9

- "Jesus went into Galilee, proclaiming the good news of God. "The time has come," he said. "The kingdom of God has come near. *Repent* and *believe the good news!*" – Mark 1:14-15
- "Yet to all who did *receive him* (Jesus), to those who *believed* in his name (Jesus), he gave the right to become children of God." – John 1:12

Receive Jesus means that you need to commit your life to Him and follow Him as your Lord & Savior. Nearly everyone wants Jesus to be their friend. Nearly everyone also wants Jesus to be their Savior and save them from their sins and the eternal punishment of hell. But many people do not really want Jesus to be their Lord. The Lord of their life. Which means to give up control and the rights to their life to Jesus. It may mean you need to give up your dreams and goals and plans, and accept Jesus' will and plans instead. It may cost you a lot. Their is a cost to follow Jesus as Lord & Savior and be His disciple (a disciple is a learner & follower of Jesus). You need to commit your life to Jesus, and commit to follow Him as your *Lord* and Savior.

If you have never trusted and received Jesus Christ as your Lord and Savior, but you are ready to do so, then you can do it right now. In order to have a restored relationship with God you need to do the 2 things that Jesus said in Mark 1:14-15, and also to receive Jesus as Lord & Savior as in John 1:12 and commit to follow Him:

1. Admit your need ("I am a sinner and I need a savior")
2. Be willing to turn from your sins (repent - Mark 1:14-15).
3. Believe with all of your heart that Jesus loves you and died for your sins and paid the price for them. Believe also that Jesus rose again from the grave after 3 days, and later ascended back to heaven. (Mark 1:14-15 and John 1:12)
4. 4. Through prayer, talk to and invite Jesus Christ to come into your life and be your Lord and Savior, and commit to follow Him in your life:

"Dear Lord, Thank you for loving me very much, and for sending Jesus to die for my sins. Lord, I have sins in my life. Please forgive me for all of my sins. And dear Lord Jesus, please come into my life, and be my Lord and Savior. I commit my life to you, to follow You and Your ways. And I repent and turn away from my sins, and I turn back to you. Please give me peace with God and eternal life in heaven. Please teach me your ways, and help me grow closer to you. In Jesus name. Amen."

If you have done these things – you truly repented of your sins, put all of your faith and hope in Jesus Christ, and received Him as your Lord & Savior and committed your life to follow Him, and you meant it sincerely with all your heart – then now you for sure have a reconciled relationship with God, peace with God and eternal life, and new life in Jesus.

"Everyone who calls on the name of the Lord will be saved." – Romans 10:13
"Those who have the Son (Jesus) have life. Those who do not have the Son do not have life. These things have I written, that you may know you have eternal life."
– I John 5:12-13

If you have prayed and repented and put your faith in Jesus, and received Him as your Lord & Savior and committed your life to Him, and meant it with all of your heart - Welcome to God's family !!!

Once you have a restored personal relationship with God through Jesus Christ, you can begin to seek to have intimate fellowship with Him and you can get to know God more and more. In Part 2 of this series we will look at what it takes for you to have intimacy with God and how you can know God personally.

PURSUING INTIMACY WITH GOD II

Week 1	HEARING GOD'S VOICE	84-85
	HINDERANCES TO HEARING GOD'S VOICE	86-87
	TRAIN / LEARN TO HEAR GOD'S VOICE	88-89
	ESSENTIALS TO LISTENING TO GOD	90
	Week 1 Study Review (p.91)	
Week 2	THE KEYS TO POWERFUL PRAYER	93
	POWERFUL PRAYER – PRAY GOD'S WORD	94
	PRAYING FOR OTHERS	95-96
	PRAY FOR THE LOST	97
	PRAYING FOR PASTORS, CHURCH, NATION	98
	FASTING & PRAYER	99
	Week 2 Study Review (p.100-101)	
Week 3	GOD WANTS TO MEET YOUR NEEDS	103-104
	GOD WANTS TO SET YOU FREE	105
	JESUS IS "THE SOURCE"	106-107
	GOD'S PROMISES	108-111
	GIVE THANKS TO GOD	112
	Week 3 Study Review (p.113)	
Week 4	FAITH IS VITAL TO INTIMACY WITH GOD	115-119
	HOW BIG IS YOUR GOD ?	120
	Week 4 Study Review (p.122)	
Week 5	WAITING ON GOD / SUBMISSION	124-131
	GOD'S SPIRITUAL GOALS FOR YOU	132
	SPIRITUAL TRAINING IN RIGHTEOUSNESS	133
	Week 5 Study Review (p.134-135)	
Week 6	PRACTICAL IDEAS FOR TIME WITH GOD	137-138
	THE KIND OF CHRISTIAN/CHURCH GOD WANTS	139-144
	Week 6 Study Review (p.145)	

HEARING (AND OBEYING) GOD'S VOICE

Hearing God's voice is by far the most important part of your prayer & fellowship time with Him. You cannot have an intimate and wonderful fellowship with God without leaning to hear God's voice and intimately communicate with Him. There can be a big difference between hearing God's voice and listening to Him. Seeking God and listening to His voice is part of having a humble and reverent heart attitude toward God.

God speaks to His people, and the Bible is full of examples. God continues to speak to His people to guide & lead them, and it is critical to learn to discern & hear God's voice.

* LISTENING TO GOD IS THE **MOST IMPORTANT PART** OF OUR TIME WITH HIM – IT'S THE ONLY WAY TO KNOW HIM AND TO BE ONE WITH HIM:

- "Be still and **know** that I am God".

- "Guard your steps when you go to the house of God. Go near to **listen** rather than to offer the sacrifice of fools." – Ecclesiastes 5:1

- " Whether you turn to the right or to the left, your ears will hear a voice behind you, saying "This is the way; Walk in it." - Isaiah 30:21

- Also read Psalm 46:10, Exodus 33:11,13,18, and Ephesians 1:17

The Biblical word for listen means: to **reverently** and **attentively** listen, with the **intent to follow or obey.** (when you do not carefully seek God through His word and through prayer and listen to Him, to God you are being irreverent)

What is the first thing that you think of when you hear the word disciple ? Do you think of guys like Matthew or Luke or John ? A true disciple is a faithful learner and follower of Jesus.

* YOU CANNOT BE A TRUE DISCIPLE (LEARNER & FOLLOWER) OF JESUS UNLESS YOU LEARN TO HEAR HIS VOICE & FOLLOW/OBEY HIM:

- " My sheep follow me **because they know my voice**... My sheep listen to my voice; I know them, and they follow me." – John 10:4, 27

- The difference between Martha and Mary (Luke 10:38-42) ... Jesus commended Mary because she took the time to humbly sit at His feet and listen to Him.

- Why did Jesus think that Mary's way was a better way than Martha's ?

* WHY SHOULD WE LISTEN TO GOD & OBEY / FOLLOW HIM ?:

- "I am the Way, the Truth, and the Life..." – John 14:6
- If you want to know the way to go, truth, and find abundant life, then you need to spend time with Jesus. You need to spend time in His word & listen to His voice.

"My son, pay attention to what I say; listen closely to my words. Do not let them out of your sight, keep them within your heart, for they are **life** to those who find them and **health** to a man's whole body."   – Proverbs 4:20-22

" Blessed are those who **hear** the Word of God **and obey** it." – Luke 11:28

Also read: Joshua 1:8, Isaiah 48:17-18, Psalm 16:8 & 11, Psalm 25:14, Proverbs 8:32-35

God has sent his wonderful Word the Bible to you so that you can learn how to live to please Him, so that you can know Him in real and personal ways, so that you can become all that He has created you to be, and for you to have the best possible life. His word is a **love letter** written personally to you.

* WHAT HAPPENS WHEN WE DON'T SEEK GOD & LISTEN AND OBEY HIM ?:
- Read Jeremiah 32:32-35, Psalm 81:8-16, and Isaiah 1:19-20

When you choose to not listen to God, you are choosing to resist and rebel against Him. When you do this, you will forfeit seeing and experiencing God's very best for you, and there will be no peace and joy and power and victory in your life.

* WHEN GOD IS YOUR "TREASURE" & "FIRST LOVE", AND YOU WANT INTIMACY WITH HIM **MORE THAN ANYTHING ELSE**, YOU WILL ALWAYS SEEK HIM AND LISTEN TO HIS VOICE:

"for where your treasure is, there your heart will be also. " - Matthew 6:21

"Seek first for His kingdom and His righteousness…"   - Matthew 6:33

"I know your deeds and your toil and perseverance, and that you cannot tolerate evil men, and you put to the test those who call themselves apostles, and they are not, and you found them *to be* false; and you have perseverance and have endured for My name's sake, and have not grown weary. But I have *this* against you, that you have left your first love." Revelation 2:2-4

"The voice of the Spirit of God is as gentle as a summer breeze -- so gentle that unless you are living in Complete Fellowship and Oneness with God, you will never hear it." – Oswald Chambers   (I Kings 19:11,12)

"Knowing God's voice comes from an INTIMATE LOVE RELATIONSHIP with God."
                                         – Experiencing God

Our **heart attitude** should always be: "Speak Lord, your servant is listening."
- I Samuel 3:9

Seeking God and hearing & listening to His voice is a heart attitude that comes from a heart of love for God, reverence for God, and a desire and passion to know Him and to please Him. It comes from a heart that has "crucified" and "denied" self, in order to have the fullest and most wonderful intimacy, fellowship, and partnership with God - He is your First Love.

LISTENING TO GOD
HINDRANCES TO HEARING GOD

There can be a big difference between hearing God's voice and listening to Him. The Biblical word listening means to reverently and attentively hear God's voice, with the intent of doing & obeying what you hear God say. Our heart needs to be right with God, with no hinderances to hearing God's voice. Seeking God and listening to His voice is part of having a humble and reverent heart attitude toward God.

Here are some hinderances to hearing God's voice that hinder us from having intimacy with God. There are many things that can cause us to not hear God's voice:

1. WE DON'T KNOW GOD VERY WELL
    - We need to be in God's word regularly to know Him.
    - God speaks to His people often in the Bible to lead and guide and instruct them
    - Many people do not know God well enough to know that He speaks to His people

2. LOW SELF ESTEEM
    - Many people don't know or feel that they are God's child & often think "Why would God want to talk to me ?"

3. GUILT (False Guilt)
    - Satan lies and gives a person a false sense of guilt.

4. TOO BUSY
    - The cares of the world crowd God out of our lives.
    - It takes quality time with God and effort to hear God's voice

5. UNBELIEF
    - You need to believe that God wants to speak to you through His Holy Spirit.

6. ANGER AT GOD
    - If you're angry at God you won't want to listen to Him.

7. SIN
    - I John 1:9 tells us that "If we confess our sins, he is faithful and just and will forgive us our sins and purify us from all unrighteousness."
    - Confession is more than just saying "I confess my sin and I sorry I sinned". Confession is agreeing with God about your sin and that you personally sinned again God, and that you intend to do something about the sin.

- There needs to be a turning away from sin (repentance) and a turn back to God. Then your fellowship with God will be restored, and you will be able to hear God's voice.

8. REBELLIOUS SPIRIT

- the opposite of knowing God is rebellion, not a lack of information
- not attentively and reverently reading God's word and not listening to Him, and living any way you want to is being rebellious towards God. It is having a hard rebellious heart.

9. YOU REJECT THE PERSON OR CIRCUMSTANCES THAT GOD IS USING TO CONFIRM WHAT HE HAS BEEN SAYING TOO YOU

- God mainly speak through His word. At times God will speak into our hearts during our prayer and quiet time with Him.
- If you think God is speaking into your heart, it should always agree with or match what you are seeing in God's word.
- God will usually use Godly people or circumstances to confirm what He is saying through His word.
- You need to pay attention to the person speaking or the circumstances, if they match up with what God is speaking through His word.

10. YOU ARE UNTRAINED TO LISTEN TO GOD

- You can learn to hear God's voice.
- It takes time but you can learn how to discern God's voice and what He is speaking to you.
- See Page 87 – Train / Learn To Listen To God

TRAIN / LEARN TO LISTEN TO GOD

Hearing God's voice is by far the most important part of your prayer & fellowship time with Him. You cannot have an intimate and wonderful fellowship with God without leaning to hear God's voice and intimately communicate with Him.

There can be a big difference between hearing God's voice and listening to Him. The Biblical word listening means to reverently and attentively hear God's voice, with the intent of doing & obeying what you hear God say. Our heart needs to be right with God, with no hinderances to hearing God's voice. Seeking God and listening to His voice is part of having a humble and reverent heart attitude toward God.

To learn to hear God's voice and discern His will and plans for you, you will need to spend time with God. You will need to read God's word, and take the time to meditate on His word. You need to spend time in prayer, and take some time to be still and listen for His voice in your heart.

You can definitely learn to hear God's voice, so keep at it and don't give up. God promises us that if we seek Him with all of our heart, we will find Him. Here is what you need to do in order to learn to hear God's voice:

* LISTENING/HEARING IS AN ACTIVE PROCESS
- You need to be willing to make the effort to learn to hear God's voice, until you accomplish your goal.
- You need to spend time with God in prayer, and read the Bible, and then meditate on His word.
- You cannot learn to hear God's will without making the effort
- Jeremiah 29:11-13 - "For I know the plans I have for you," declares the LORD, "plans to prosper you and not to harm you, plans to give you hope and a future. Then you will call on me and come and pray to me, and I will listen to you. You will seek me and find me when you seek me with all your heart."

* YOU NEED TO TAKE TIME TO LISTEN
- It takes time to get to know God and His voice. Knowing God is a lifelong process.
- It will not take you a lifetime to learn to hear God's voice and discern His leading and will, but it will take time and effort.

* MEDITATE ON GOD'S WORD AND ASK QUESTIONS:
- What is God saying to you ?
- How does what I sense in my Prayer time, or in my Circumstances, or what Godly People are telling me *confirm* what I read and hear from God's word ?
- How can I do / apply / obey/ follow what I am reading & hearing from God ?

* ANTICIPATE AND EXPECT GOD TO SPEAK (IT'S THE BIBLICAL PATTERN)
- Hebrews 1:1-2 "God, after He spoke long ago to the fathers in the prophets in many portions and in many ways, in these last days has spoken to us in His Son, whom He appointed heir of all things, through whom also He made the world."
- God spoke to many of His people in the Bible, to lead them, or guide them, or teach them, or rebuke them.
- You need to know that God wants to speak to you also, and you should expect Him to.

* BE READY TO RESPOND TO WHAT YOU HEAR (WILLING AND OBEDIENT)
- There is a big difference between hearing God's voice and listening. In the Bible, to listen means to have a humble, soft, and willing heart that is ready to obey or follow... even before you hear what God is saying.
- James 1:22 - "But prove yourselves doers of the word, and not merely hearers who delude themselves."

* LOOK FOR A CONFIRMATION (PRAYER/ CIRCUMSTANCES/ GODLY PEOPLE)
- This is an important step, especially if you sense God leading you to do something to serve Him. Especially if it involves making changes in your life.
- When God was making it clear that He was calling us to sell my business (and house...) and become full time, self funded missionaries in Brazil, we were not about to do major things like that without asking Him for confirmations.
- We prayed asked that God would clearly confirm that we heard His voice and leading correctly.
- God answered and confirmed that it was His will and calling for us to go and serve in Brazil. He confirmed this in several different ways, using our circumstances, what some Godly people were saying, and what we sensed in our hearts during extended prayer times of seeking Him.
- We were absolutely sure of what God what leading us to do because of His confirmations.
- Because we completely surrendered all to God and were willing to do whatever He wanted, God also gave us a very clear vision and idea of what and how He wanted us to do in our missions ministry.

God speaks through: His Word, your Prayer Time, Circumstances, & Godly people. He will use what you sense in your heart during your prayer time &/or your circumstances &/or what Godly people tell you to confirm what He has been saying through His word. Everything must match up with God's word.

You need to be careful with trying to interpret your circumstances by themselves, because often times our feeling and what we think we see going on can be deceptive. Also, you will hear many different things from many different people. Even people in church that mean well can tell you things that do not match what God is trying to tell you, or with how He is trying to lead you. We heard different things from various people at church, and even a pastor, that were contrary to what God was saying to us.

God speaks through: His Word, Prayer, Circumstances, & Godly people.

ESSENTIALS TO LISTENING TO GOD

1. TIME & EFFORT

　- You need to take time to seek God and listen to Him

"If you have so much business to attend to that you have no time to pray, depend upon it, you have more business on hand than God ever intended you should have."
- D.L. Moody

2. STILLNESS

- "Be still and know that I am God." - Psalm 46:10
- You need to have quiet and stop all you are doing
- You need to concentrate and focus on God

3. SECLUSION

　- You need to get alone with God

4. SILENCE

　- You need to let God do the talking before you speak and pray

5. SELF-CONTROL

　- Be devoted to God; be disciplines; stick with it and do not give up

6. HUMILITY & SUBMISSION　(John 10:27; Isaiah 1:19-20; Exodus 33:13)

　- You need to have a soft & willing & obedient heart
　- Be willing to do whatever God tells you to do
　- Be willing to be whatever God wants you to be
　- Be willing to go wherever God tells you to go

"God gives the gift of humility, which brings a softness of heart – a gift that will always cause you to listen to God."　　　– Oswald Chambers

"Lord, send me anywhere - only go with me; Lay any burden on me - only sustain me; Sever all ties, except the one that binds me to yourself." - David Livingstone

YOU CAN'T BE INTIMATE WITH GOD AND HAVE THE FULLEST POSSIBLE FELLOWSHIP & PARTNERSHIP WITH HIM UNLESS YOU **SUBMIT ALL** TO HIM AND BECOME ONE WITH HIM

WEEK 1 STUDY REVIEW (Pages 84-90)

- READ **LUKE 10:38-42** ; ARE YOU MORE LIKE MARY OR MARTHA IN THE WAY YOU HANDLE YOUR PERSONAL RELATIONSHIP WITH JESUS ?:

___ Martha: busy, busy, busy, trying to do her very best to do things for Jesus (but being so busy doing things <u>for</u> Jesus that she did not take time to be <u>with</u> Jesus, and hear from Him, and get to <u>know</u> Jesus by Him revealing to her who He really is.

___ Mary: she saw and understood the "one thing" she really needed -- a personal and real relationship with Jesus, so she made sure she spent time with Him, and listened to Him, and got to <u>know</u> Him. She then served Him out of love & devotion & passion for Him.

- REVIEW PAGE 84 & 85: CHOOSE THE STATEMENTS ABOUT HEARING GOD'S VOICE AND SEEING HIS ACTIVITY IN YOUR LIFE THAT ARE TRUE:

___ It's all about WHAT you do (go to church, pray, read the Bible, meditate on it,...) rather than also being about How you do it and Why you do it (what's in your heart).

___ When we see Jesus for who He really is (Creator and Lord and Owner of all) we will be more reverent and attentive to hearing Him and following Him.

___ When Jesus becomes our "treasure" and we value and desire Him more than anything else, we will ALWAYS hear His voice and see His activity, unless our fellowship with Him is broken by sin.

___ "God's voice" is the Holy Spirit trying to speak to you and lead you and reveal to you who God is, and reveal His ways and His activity and His plans for your life.

___ You can hear God's voice & see His activity without being in close fellowship with Him.

- REVIEW PAGE 86-87: MARK T FOR TRUE OR F FOR FALSE:

___ One of the main reasons people do not hear God's voice is that they do not know God and that He still personally speaks to and leads His children.

___ Sadly in the church of America, the cares & riches of the world have captured many people's minds & hearts, and are too busy to spend time with God and hear His voice.

___ You need to believe and trust that God wants to personally speak to you and lead you.

___ You need to be a pastor or at least a deacon in order to hear God's voice.

___ You have to go to seminary in order to learn how to hear God's voice.

___ You can learn to hear and recognize God's voice and His leading in your life.

___ You can take a short cut and bypass the time it takes to build your personal relationship with God in order to learn to hear His voice and to see and know Him.

___ You need to learn to anticipate and expect God to speak to you and reveal Himself.

- REVIEW PAGE 90: WHICH ARE ESSENTIALS TO HEARING GOD'S VOICE AND SEEING HIS ACTIVITY IN YOUR LIFE ?:

___ You need to take the time to get to know God and to listen to Him and watch for Him.

___ You need to get even busier at church so that you can earn God's favor and blessings.

___ You need to be still and be quiet, humble yourself and ask God to reveal Himself to you.

___ You need to read God's word over & over again until you figure it out.

___ You need a soft, humble, teachable, willing, and obedient heart, and you need to **submit** yourself and your life to God, and be willing to do or be whatever He wants.

Get face to face with God and prayerfully review this week's material. Ask God to show you how you can be closer to Him and more one with Him

THE KEYS TO A POWERFUL PRAYER LIFE

GOD'S WORD REVEALS THE KEYS TO HAVING A POWERFUL PRAYER LIFE, AND CLOSE FELLOWSHIP & ONENESS WITH GOD, AND A PARTNERSHIP WITH HIM (KOINANIA FELLOWSHIP in 1 Corinthians 1:9)

1. CLOSE & RIGHT FELLOWSHIP WITH GOD (JESUS IS YOUR 1ST LOVE)
- James 5:16b
- Proverbs 21:21
- John 14, 15
- Matthew 6:33 ; 22:37-40
- Deuteronomy 28:1-14
- Revelation 2:1-4

2. YOU NEED TO CONTINUALLY PRAY AND TRUST GOD, AND DEPEND ON HIM FOR EVERYTHING
- James 4:2b
- Jeremiah 33:3
- Matthew 7:7-11
- I John 3:21-22

3. SUBMISSION & PRAY ACCORDING TO GOD'S HEART/ DESIRES / WILL
(HOW CAN WE DO THIS ? LEARN TO PRAY GOD'S WORD- PAGE 89)
- I John 5:14-15
- Luke 11:1-2
- Isaiah 30:18
- James 4:3
- Psalm 34:8
- Exodus 33:17-19; 34:5-8

4. EXPECT GOD TO ANSWER (FAITH)
(WHEN WE PRAY ACCORDING TO GOD'S HEART/ WILL/ WORD, WE CAN **EXPECT** ANSWERS - IN HIS WAY & IN HIS TIME)
- James 1:6-7
- I John 5:14-15
- Hebrews 11:1, 6
- I John 3:21-22

God wants to take care of all of your needs & bless you, give you an honorable & fulfilling life, and give you the privilege of joining him in his kingdom work – all for his glory. (I Chronicles 4:9,10 ; Matt. 6:33 ; John 10:10; 15:5-8 ; Ephesians 3:20)

"During the days of Jesus' life on earth, he offered up prayers and petitions with loud cries and tears to the one who could save him from death, and he was heard because of his **reverent submission**."- Hebrews 5:7

- "... yet not my will, **but yours be done**." - Luke 22:42

"One of those days Jesus went out to a mountain side to pray, and **spent the entire night praying to God**. When morning came, he called his disciples to him and chose twelve of them." - Luke 6:12-13

When we begin to live and pray like Jesus did, we will see God's mighty power in our lives and churches and nation and world

POWERFUL PRAYER: PRAY GOD'S WORD

GOD'S WORD IS A SPIRITUAL WEAPON ("SWORD OF THE SPIRIT") (EPHESIANS 6)

You can **expect answers** when you pray according to God's will (I John 5:14-15). The best way to do this is to pray God's Word. Here are some examples:

- " GIVE ME A HEART TO KNOW YOU " - Jeremiah 24:7

- "LET US KNOW THE TRUTH AND SET US FREE." - John 8:32

- "OPEN MY EYES THAT I MAY SEE WONDERFUL THINGS IN YOUR LAW."
  - Psalm 119:18

- "CREATE IN ME A PURE HEART, O GOD, AND RENEW A STEADFAST (RIGHT) SPIRIT WITHIN ME." - Psalm 51:10

- "CLEANSE THOU ME FROM SECRET FAULTS." ("FORGIVE MY HIDDEN FAULTS.")
  - Psalm 19:12

- "I DO BELIEVE; HELP ME OVERCOME MY UNBELIEF." - Mark 9:24

- "HEAR MY VOICE WHEN I CALL, O LORD; BE MERCIFUL TO ME & ANSWER ME."
  - Psalm 27:7

- "... YOUR FACE LORD I WILL SEEK." - Psalm 27:8

- "TEACH ME YOUR WAY, O LORD; LEAD ME IN A STRAIGHT PATH." - Psalm 27:11

- "TEACH ME YOUR WAYS, SO I MAY KNOW YOU & CONTINUE TO FIND FAVOR WITH YOU." - Exodus 33:13

- " LORD, BE MY FIRST LOVE." - Revelation 2:4

- " **NOT MY WILL**, BUT YOUR WILL BE DONE." - Luke 22:42

- OTHER PRAYERS:
    - POWER TO BOLDLY SHARE THE GOSPEL   Acts 4:29-31
    - FOR A BROKEN & HUMBLE SPIRIT   Psalm 51:17
    - FOR A SERVANT'S HEART   Mark 10:44-45
    - TO BE ALERT TO SATAN'S ATTACKS & WAYS   I John 4:4
    - TO BE CONFORMED TO JESUS' LIKENESS Romans 8:29
    - TO BE **ONE WITH GOD** LIKE JESUS IS   John 17:22
    - TO **KNOW GOD** MORE & MORE   Ephesians 1:17
    - TO BE FILLED WITH THE HOLY SPIRIT   Epphesians 5:18

When you yield yourself to God & His will, and pray and live according to His will and His word, then you can expect answers to your prayers, and expect to see God display His glory and power !!

PRAYING FOR OTHERS

* A RIGHTEOUS PERSON'S PRAYERS WILL BE POWERFUL & EFFECTIVE (JAMES 5:16b) (OUR HEART MUST BE RIGHT WITH GOD CONCERNING THE PERSON / PEOPLE WE ARE PRAYING FOR IN ORDER TO BE EFFECTIVE)

* GOD WILL NOT HONOR OR BLESS A SELFISH LIFESTYLE

   - "DO NOTHING OUT OF SELFISH AMBITION OR VAIN CONCEIT, BUT IN HUMILITY CONSIDER OTHERS BETTER THAN YOURSELVES. EACH OF YOU SHOULD LOOK NOT ONLY TO YOUR INTERESTS, BUT ALSO TO THE INTERESTS OF OTHERS."
                        -Philippians 2:3-4

   - I SAMUEL 12:23 (IS IT A SIN TO NOT PRAY FOR OTHERS ?)

* IT IS GOD'S WILL FOR US NOT ONLY TO PRAY FOR OTHERS, BUT TO HELP OTHERS WITH THEIR BURDENS AND NEEDS AS WELL:

   - "CARRY EACH OTHER'S BURDENS, AND IN THIS WAY YOU WILL FULFILL THE LAW OF CHRIST."   - Galatians 6:2

   - " ... ALWAYS KEEP ON PRAYING FOR THE SAINTS."
                        - Ephesians 6:18

* ASK THE LORD TO DIRECT YOU TO SOMEONE THAT NEEDS YOUR HELP; HE WILL DO IT. (THERE IS JOY IN SERVING OTHERS)

* DON'T SIMPLY PRAY FOR SOMEONE; ASK GOD WHAT YOU CAN DO FOR THAT PERSON, AND WHAT HE WOULD HAVE YOU TO DO.

* PRAYING FOR OTHERS / WHO TO PRAY FOR ?:
    - THOSE THAT PERSECUTE YOU & HURT YOU (JERKS) (Matthew 5:44)
    - PRAY FOR THE LOST   - PEOPLE AWAY FROM THE LORD
    - PRAY FOR THE SICK   - PRAY FOR THE LONELY
    - FINANCIAL DIFFICULTIES   - THE POOR & NEEDY
    - PERSECUTED CHRISTIANS   - DISCOURAGED/DEPRESSED
    - YOUR PASTORS, YOUR CHURCH, & GOVERNMENT LEADERS (PAGE 39)

* SPIRITUAL PRAYERS FOR OTHERS (Colossians 1:9-12; Ephesians 1:15-19) (Philippians 1:9-11; Colossians 4:2-6; Nehemiah 1:5-11; Matthew 6:9-13)

God's word shows that He expects you to be in prayer on behalf of others. His word also shows that He wants you to not only pray for others, but to be involved in ministering to others and to be involved in reaching out to the lost. When you spend time with God and pray for others in His presence, God will touch and change your heart and will make your heart more and more like His towards others, and especially towards the lost.

WHY DID GOD LET "JERKS" BE IN THE WORLD ANYWAY ?

"Love your enemies, and pray for those who persecute you, that you may be sons of your Father in heaven. ... Be perfect, therefore, as your heavenly Father is perfect." (Matthew 5:44, 48)

"But if you do not forgive men their sins, your Father will not forgive your sins." (Matthew 6:15)

"Dear friends, since God so loved us, we also ought to love one another. No one has seen God, but if we love one another, God lives in us and His love is made complete in us." (I John 4:11, 12)

GOD'S GUIDELINES FOR PRAYING FOR THE LOST

1. PRAY FOR THEM BY NAME.

2. ASK OTHERS TO PRAY FOR THEM.

3. PRAY FOR GOD TO ARRANGE A CONTACT BETWEEN A CHRISTIAN (YOURSELF ?) AND THE LOST PERSON.
   - SOMEONE WHO CARES & HAS A BURDEN & LOVE FOR THE LOST.
   - SOMEONE WHO WILL SHARE THE GOSPEL & SHOW THEM GOD'S LOVE

4. PRAY THAT THEY WILL SEE GOD FOR WHO HE REALLY IS. (Ephesians 1:17)

5. PRAY FOR THEIR CONVICTION BY THE HOLY SPIRIT (John 16:8)

6. PRAY FOR THEM TO GET A SEEKING HEART. (Romans 3:10,11)

7. PRAY FOR GOD TO DRAW THEM TO HIMSELF. (John 12:32)

8. PRAY IN FAITH FOR THEIR SALVATION.

9. PRAY IN THANKSGIVING FOR THEIR SALVATION AND PRAISE GOD FOR IT:

"THIS IS THE CONFIDENCE WE HAVE IN APPROACHING GOD; THAT IF WE ASK ANYTHING ACCORDING TO HIS WILL, HE HEARS US; AND IF WE KNOW THAT HE HEARS US- WHATEVER WE ASK- WE KNOW THAT WE HAVE WHAT WE ASKED OF HIM."   - I John 5:14,15

"THIS IS GOOD, AND PLEASES GOD OUR SAVIOR, WHO WANTS ALL MEN TO BE SAVED AND TO COME TO A KNOWLEDGE OF THE TRUTH." I Timothy 2:1-4

* "BUT I'VE PRAYED & PRAYED &AND THEY'RE STILL NOT SAVED":

"THE LORD IS NOT SLOW IN KEEPING HIS PROMISE, AS SOME UNDERSTAND SLOWNESS; HE IS PATIENT WITH YOU, NOT WANTING ANYONE TO PERISH, BUT EVERYONE TO COME TO REPENTANCE."   - 2 PETER 3:9

(D.L. Moody, a great man of God, prayed for over 60 years for 2 of his childhood friends - one was finally saved during his last sermon and one was saved shortly after he died)

* **NEVER GIVE UP !!!** (Luke 18:1, Galatians 6:9)

"Prayer is not the least you can do for someone, prayer is the **most** you can do for someone. - Billy Graham

"Prayer is the mightiest force in the world." - Billy Graham

PRAY FOR YOUR PASTORS

PRAY **DAILY** FOR YOUR PASTOR & THE CHURCH STAFF:
- FOR A CLOSE RELATIONSHIP WITH GOD & A COMMITTED PRAYER LIFE.
- FOR SPIRITUAL STRENGTH TO FIGHT OFF SATAN'S ATTACKS.
- FOR HUMILITY; A TEACHABLE SPIRIT; A SERVANT'S HEART. (Exodus 33:13)
- FOR A SOFT & OBEDIENT & LISTENING HEART. ("AFTER GOD'S OWN HEART")
- FOR PHYSICAL & EMOTIONAL STRENGTH TO DO THEIR JOB.
- FOR THE HOLY SPIRIT'S POWER FOR MINISTRY. (Philippians 4:13)
- FOR BOLDNESS TO DO THE THINGS GOD WANTS DONE. (Ephesians 6:19-20)
- FOR WISDOM & GUIDANCE.
- FOR INSIGHT INTO GOD'S WORD. (John 16:13)
- FOR VISION OF GOD'S WILL & PLAN FOR THE CHURCH. (Proverbs 29:18)
- THAT GOD WILL SPEAK THROUGH YOUR PASTOR IN HIS SERMONS.
- FOR GOOD SPIRITUAL & EMOTIONAL & PHYSICAL HEALTH

PRAY FOR YOUR CHURCH

- PRAY SPECIFICALLY FOR DIFFERENT MINISTRIES THAT YOU HAVE AN INTEREST IN OR A BURDEN FOR (MISSIONS, YOUTH, CHOIR, MEN'S, ...)
- PRAY THAT GOD WILL RAISE UP SPIRIT-FILLED LEADERS.
- PRAY THAT GOD WILL PROVIDE HIS POWER & USE US TO REACH THE LOST.
- PRAY THAT THE WORK OF THE CHURCH MAY BE DONE IN HIS POWER
- PRAY THAT GOD WILL TAKE AWAY ANY STRIFE PRESENT IN THE CHURCH BODY AND BRING UNITY. (JOHN 17)
- PRAY FOR YOUR SUNDAY SCHOOL TEACHER.
- PRAY FOR YOUR CHURCH TO BE A PRAYING CHURCH (Isaiah 56:7; Luke 19:46)

PRAY FOR OUR NATION & GOVERNMENT LEADERS
(I Timothy 2:1-3) (Proverbs 29:2)

- PRAY THAT GOD WILL SEND MORE GODLY LEADERS TO RUN OUR COUNTRY.
- PRAY THAT GOD WILL GIVE OUR LEADERS WISDOM.
- PRAY THAT GOD WILL CHANGE OUR COUNTRY'S MORALS (PORNOGRAPHY, ABORTION, HOMOSEXUALITY, DRUGS, CRIME, DIVORCE, ...)
- PRAY THAT GOD WILL CONVICT & CHANGE US (CHURCH OF AMERICA)

" IF MY PEOPLE, WHO ARE CALLED BY MY NAME, WILL 1) HUMBLE THEMSELVES, 2) AND **PRAY**, 3) AND **SEEK MY FACE**, 4) AND **TURN** FROM THEIR WICKED WAYS THEN WILL I HEAR FROM HEAVEN AND WILL FORGIVE THEIR SIN, AND WILL HEAL THEIR LAND."   - 2 Chronicles 7:14

* SEE PRAYER AND FASTING INFORMATION – PAGE 94
- the next page shows some practical tips for Fasting & Prayer
 - fasting shows God that you are very serious about the things you are praying for, about getting right with God, and about your relationship and fellowship with Him.

7 BASIC STEPS TO SUCCESSFUL FASTING & PRAYER
(www.fastingprayer.com)

1. SET YOUR OBJECTIVE: (OUR NATION NEEDS GOD)
- Are you fasting for spiritual renewal, guidance, healing, solutions to problems,... ?
- Ask the Holy Spirit to clarify His leading & objectives for your prayer fast.

2. MAKE YOUR COMMITMENT AHEAD OF TIME:
- Pray about the kind of fast you should undertake
- How long will you fast -- 1 meal, 1 day, 1 week, 1 month, 40 days ?
(beginners should start slowly, building up to longer fasts)
- What physical or social activities will you restrict ?
- How much time each day will you devote to prayer & God's Word

2. PREPARE YOURSELF SPIRITUALLY:
- The foundation of fasting & prayer is repentance; unconfessed sin will hinder prayer.
- Ask God to help you make a comprehensive list of your sins.
- Confess every sin the Holy Spirit calls to your attention; accept God's forgiveness.
- Seek forgiveness from all whom you have offended.
- Forgive all who have hurt you or offended you.
- Ask God to fill you with His Holy Spirit and give you strength.
- Surrender your life FULLY to Jesus Christ as your Lord and Master.
- Meditate on the attributes and character of God and His love.

3. PREPARE YOURSELF PHYSICALLY:
- Consult you physician first (if an extended fast)
- Prepare your body. Eat smaller meals before starting a fast. Avoid high-fat and sugar.
- Eat fruit and vegetables for 2 days prior to starting a long fast.
- Limit your physical activities during the fast; exercise only moderately.

5. WHILE YOU FAST- BE DISCIPLINED:
- Begin your day in praise & worship. (pray for His vision for your life & power to do it)
- Read & meditate on God's Word.
- Avoid television and other distractions that may dampen your spiritual focus.
- Put yourself on a dietary routine - a daily schedule of water & juices (recommended fruit juices include apple, grapefruit, papaya, watermelon, lemon, and grape; recommended vegetable juices include carrot, beet, celery, cabbage, other leafy green vegetables)
- Avoid caffeinated drinks if possible, and chewing gum or mints. These stimulate digestive action in your stomach.

4. END YOUR FAST GRADUALLY:
- Begin eating gradually. Do not eat solid foods immediately after a long fast. Try fruit,...

5. EXPECT RESULTS AND ANSWERS TO PRAYER:
- If you sincerely humble yourself, pray, seek God's face, and repent-- you will experience a heightened awareness of God's presence & love; the Lord will give you fresh, new spiritual insights; your confidence & faith in God will grow; you will see answers/results.

WEEK 2 STUDY REVIEW (Pages 93-99)

- PLACE A T FOR TRUE OR F FOR FALSE CONCERNING HOW TO HAVE A POWERFUL PRAYER LIFE (PAGE 93):

___ The key to praying powerfully is getting whatever you want by being persistent.
___ You need a close and right fellowship with God (your heart needs to be right with Him and Jesus need to be your 1st Love) in order to have a powerful prayer life (see James 5:16b)
___ If you pray according to God's will <u>and</u> you have a right relationship with Him, you can **know** that God hears you, and you can **know** that God will give you what you ask for.
___ Some of the best and most powerful prayers are in the Bible.
___ In God's eyes, Jesus had one of the all time best prayers- "not my will, but your will be done"

- READ **JAMES 5:16b** & THE TOP OF PAGE 93; CHOOSE THE TRUE STATEMENTS:

___ All Christians' prayers are powerful and effective.
___ A Christian who has close & right fellowship with God will have a powerful prayer life.
___ Your heart has to be right with God concerning the person you are praying for (you have to have the same heart of love for the person that God has) in order to pray powerfully and effectively for that person; otherwise God will not honor or even listen to your prayers.
___ What matters most is that you are praying, not that your fellowship is right with God.

- READ **I SAMUEL 12:23**; IS IT A SIN (ESPECIALLY FOR A CHURCH LEADER) TO NOT PRAY FOR OTHERS ? ___ YES ___ NO ___ THAT DOESN'T SOUND RIGHT

- WHO SHOULD WE BE PRAYING FOR ? (See page 95):

___ Those who hurt or wrong or persecute you (Matt. 5:44)   ___ The "jerks" we know (p.96)
___ Always keep on praying for the saints (each other)   ___ The sick, needy, lonely,...
___ People who are obviously evil and enemies of God   ___ Discouraged people
___ Christians who have turned away from the Lord   ___ Unsaved family, neighbors,...

- WHICH OF THESE DO YOU THINK IS TRUE:

___ One of the reasons that God wants you to pray for those that hurt you or wrong you ("the jerks") is so that He will be able to <u>change them</u> to how you think they should be.
___ God wants you to pray for those that hurt you or wrong you ("the jerks") so that He can <u>change you and your heart</u> towards other people, even "jerks" -- so you can be forgiving, compassionate, kind,... and so you can truly love others like He does.

- REVIEW PAGE 97; WHAT ARE SOME OF THE KEY THINGS YOU NEED TO ASK GOD TO DO SO THAT LOST PEOPLE YOU KNOW CAN COME TO KNOW JESUS AS THEIR LORD AND SAVIOR ?:

___ Pray that they will be able to see God for who He really is.
___ Pray for God to convict them and show them their sinfulness and their need for Jesus.
___ Pray for them to get a seeking heart (an interest in God and in spiritual matters)
___ Pray for God to draw them to Himself and His great love for them.
___ Pray for them specifically by name.
___ Pray in <u>faith</u> for them, <u>expecting</u> God to do everything He can to touch them & save them (if you have a right relationship with God and you pray according to God's will, you can **know** that He hears your prayer, and you can **know** that you have what you prayer for).

- REVIEW PAGE 98 AND ANSWER THE FOLLOWING QUESTIONS:

___ Does God want us to pray for our pastors, leaders,...?
___ Do we need to pray for God's leading & power for our church ?
___ Does God want us to pray for our president & nation's leaders ?
___ According to **2 Chronicles 7:14** -- in order for God to "heal our nation", do we American Christians need to change (humble ourselves, pray, seek, turn) or do the unsaved people ?

Get face to face with God and prayerfully review this week's material. Ask God to show you how you can be closer to Him and more one with Him

GOD WANTS TO MEET YOUR NEEDS & BLESS YOU

God's Word encourages us to pray continually, and to ask God for the things we need. He wants us to pray about all areas of our lives, and ask Him for His help and guidance, and His blessings. He wants us to ask and then experience His goodness and faithfulness in real and personal ways, so that we will know Him... not just know about Him.

- " TASTE AND SEE THAT THE LORD IS GOOD."   - Psalm 34:8
- God is encouraging us to try Him out, to "taste" and experience that He is good.

"Ho! Every one who thirsts, come to the waters; And you who have no money come, buy and eat. Come, buy wine and milk Without money and without cost. "Why do you spend money for what is not bread, and your wages for what does not satisfy ? Listen carefully to Me, and eat what is good, and delight yourself in abundance. "Incline your ear and come to Me. Listen, that you may live; And I will make an everlasting covenant with you, according to the faithful mercies shown to David."   - Isaiah 55:1-3
- God is not only talking about physical needs like food and drink here. He is encouraging people to come to Him for all needs (emotional, personal, spiritual), and especially for our greatest need: a restored personal relationship with Him

When Moses asked to see God's glory (to experience more of God), here is what God showed Him:
- "Then Moses said, "I pray You, show me Your glory!" And He said, "I Myself will make all My **goodness** pass before you, and will proclaim the name of the LORD before you; and I will be **gracious** to whom I will be gracious, and will show **compassion** on whom I will show compassion."   - Exodus 33:18-19

"So I say to you, ask, and it will be given to you; seek, and you will find; knock, and it will be opened to you. For everyone who asks, receives; and he who seeks, finds; and to him who knocks, it will be opened. Now suppose one of you fathers is asked by his son for a fish; he will not give him a snake instead of a fish, will he? Or *if* he is asked for an egg, he will not give him a scorpion, will he? If you then, being evil, know how to give good gifts to your children, how much more will *your* heavenly Father give the Holy Spirit to those who ask Him?"   - Luke 11:9-13

"I have set the LORD continually before me; Because He is at my right hand, I will not be shaken. Therefore my heart is glad and my glory rejoices;
My flesh also will dwell securely. For You will not abandon my soul to Sheol;
Nor will You allow Your Holy One to undergo decay. You will make known to me the path of life; In Your presence is fullness of joy; In Your right hand there are pleasures forever."
-Psalm 16:8-11
- King David submitted His life to God and enjoyed God's presence and fellowship in His life. He also enjoyed God's protection and security. He also discovered the joy that comes with continually being in God's presence and spending time with Him.
- Verse 10 is also a prophecy concerning the coming Messiah Jesus

"You have also given me the shield of Your salvation, and Your right hand upholds me; And Your [q]gentleness makes me great. You enlarge my steps under me, and my feet have not slipped."   -Psalm 18:35

Here are some examples of the things that God wants you to pray and talk to Him about:

1. YOU & YOUR FAMILY'S NEEDS
- **SPIRITUAL** (Ephesians 3:14-19) (INTIMACY & ONENESS WITH GOD, TRUTH, WISDOM, GUIDANCE, FAITH, JOY, CONTENTMENT, PEACE, PATIENCE, REST, HOLINESS,...)
- EMOTIONAL (SELF ESTEEM/WORTH, SECURITY, LOVE, ACCEPTANCE,...)
- PERSONAL   (FRIENDSHIP,...)
- PHYSICAL   (SAFETY, HEALTH, FOOD, CLOTHES, SHELTER,...)
- FINANCIAL (BILLS, DEBTS,...) (GUIDANCE, WISDOM...)
- YOUR GOALS & DESIRES ? (Proverbs 19:21 ; Psalm 33:10-11; Psalm 37:4)

(The order above is the reverse of how many people typically pray)

(Other verses: Psalm 119:36,37 ; Psalm 47:4 ; Proverbs 30:8,9 ; Numbers 6:24-26)

2. YOUR MARRIAGE, FAMILY,...
- ASK GOD TO BLESS YOUR RELATIONSHIPS.
- ASK GOD TO GUIDE YOU TO BE THE HUSBAND/WIFE HE WANTS YOU TO BE.
- ASK GOD TO BLESS YOUR COMMUNICATION.
- ASK GOD TO SOLVE ANY PROBLEMS (LARGE OR SMALL).
- ASK GOD TO BLESS YOUR SPOUSE'S & FAMILY'S SPIRITUAL GROWTH.
- YOUR CHILDREN:
  * PRAY FOR THEIR SALVATION !!!
  - PRAY FOR THEIR LONG-TERM SPIRITUAL HEALTH, AND THAT THEY MAY TURN OUT THE WAY GOD WANTS THEM TO (AS CHRISTIANS WHO LOVE GOD FULLY, AND ARE DEDICATED TO SERVING HIM & LIVING FOR HIM). (Philippians 1:6)
  - PRAY FOR THEIR SPIRITUAL & EMOTIONAL & SOCIAL ... GROWTH.
  - PRAY FOR GOD'S BEST FOR THEIR LIVES (MINISTRY, CAREER, MARRIAGE,...)

3. HURTS, EMOTIONAL PROBLEMS, SIN...:
- "BRING MY SOUL OUT OF PRISON THAT I MAY PRAISE YOUR NAME" - Psalm 142:7 - "LET GOD SET YOU & YOUR SOUL FREE" - PAGE 100

4. OTHER THINGS TO PRAY FOR & TRUST GOD WITH:
- TROUBLES   Psalm 34:6 , Psalm 46:1 , Psalm 50:15
- FEARS   Deuteronomy 31:8 , Psalm 34:4 , Isaiah 41:10

* GOD CARES ABOUT YOUR LIFE & WANTS THE BEST FOR YOU:
- I Peter 5:7   - Psalm 62:8   - Hebrews 4:16   - Isaiah 48:17,18
- Mark 10:51   - 2 Samuel 12:7-9   - Jeremiah 29:11   - Isaiah 58:11

* the **PRAYER OF JABEZ** - "Jabez was more honorable than his brothers, and his mother named him Jabez saying, "Because I bore *him* with pain." Now Jabez called on the God of Israel, saying, "Oh that You would **bless me** indeed and enlarge my border, and that Your hand might be with me, and that You would keep *me* from harm that *it* may not pain me!" And God granted him what he requested." - I Chronicles 4:9,10

LET JESUS SET YOU & YOUR SOUL FREE
Only Jesus can set your heart/mind/soul free

"Bring my soul out of prison, that I may praise your name." - Psalm 142:7

"Don't you know that when you offer yourselves to someone to obey him as slaves, you are slaves to the one whom you obey."

"The thief (Satan) comes only to steal and kill and destroy; I have come that they may have life, and have it to the full. I am The good shepherd." - John 10:10

"Now the Lord is the Spirit, and where the Spirit of the Lord there is FREEDOM." - 2 Corinthians 3:17

"For though we walk in the flesh, we do not war according to flesh. For the weapons of our warfare are not of the flesh, but divinely powerful for the demolition of strongholds."

"The Lord has annointed Me to bring good news to the afflicted. ...to proclaim liberty to captives and freedom to prisoners."

INSECURITY   UNFORGIVENESS

          CONTROL

                  JEALOUSY

FAILURE   NOT CONTENT

                  DISCOURAGEMENT

IMAGE   LEGALISM (SELF EFFORT)

                  SPIRITUAL PRIDE

SELF PITY   WORLDLINESS

                  FEAR

GOD WANTS YOU TO **YIELD** YOUR HEART/MIND/SOUL & LIFE TO HIM, SO HE CAN **FILL YOU** WITH **HIS GLORY** (His Love, Joy, Peace, Patience, Power...)
(THE "FULLNESS OF CHRIST"- **Ephesians 3:19, 4:11-13, 5:18 ; John 7:38**)

JESUS – "THE SAVIOR", "THE HEALER", "THE SOURCE" "THE WAY, THE TRUTH, THE LIFE"

Whatever you are lacking or whatever is missing in your life, Jesus wants to give to you in overflowing measure . Go to Jesus with your emptiness, or your need or your hurt or your problem– He is **The Source**, and He wants to help you.

Abundant, Full Life:
- "I have come that they may have <u>life</u>, and have it to the <u>full</u> (abundant life)." - John 10:10
- "that you may be <u>filled</u> with the <u>fullness of God</u> - Ephesians 3:19 (full of Jesus' love, joy, peace, patience, kindness,...)
- " Whoever believes in me, streams o f <u>living water</u> (abundant life) will flow from within him." - John 7:38

Fulfillment, Purpose, Satisfaction:
- " I am the bread of life. He who comes to me will never go hungry... and never go thirsty." - John 6:35
- "... the one who feeds o n me (fills their heart & soul with Jesus) will <u>live</u> because of me." - John 6:57
- "Come, all you who are thirsty, come to the waters... why spend your labor on what does not satisfy ? Listen to me, and eat what is good, and your soul will delight in the richest of fare. Give ear and come to me; hear me, that your soul may live . - Isaiah 55:1-3
- " ... I will guide you continually and satisfy your needs..." - Isaiah 58:11

Direction, Guidance, Wisdom:
- "For I know the <u>plans</u> I have for you, declares the Lord, plans to <u>prosper</u> you and not to harm you, plans to give you <u>hope</u> and a <u>future</u>." - Jeremiah 29:11
- "... I will <u>guide</u> you continually..." - Isaiah 58:11
- "Trust in the Lord with all of your heart, and lean not on your own understanding; in all your ways acknowledge him, and he will make your paths straight."
- " If any of you lacks <u>wisdom,</u> he should ask Go d who gives generously" - James 1:5
- " <u>I am</u> the Way... " - John 14:6

Love:
- "God so <u>loved</u> the world that he gave his one and only Son ..."   - John 3:16
- "God demonstrated his own <u>love</u> for us in this: while we were still sinners, Christ died for us. - Roman 5:8
- "...how wide & long & high and deep is the <u>love</u> of Christ for you." - Ephesians 3:18
- "God has poured out his love into our hearts by the Holy Spirit." - Rom ans 5:3

Joy:
- "I have told you this so that my joy may be in you and that your joy may be complete" - John 15:11
- "I have set the Lo rd always before m e. Because he is at m y right hand, I will not be shaken. Therefore my heart is glad and my tongue rejoices... you will fill me with joy in your presence..." - Psalm 16:8-9,11
- " The precepts of the Lord are right, giving joy to the heart." - Psalm 19:8

Peace:
- "You will keep in perfect peace him whose m ind is steadfast (fixed on you), because he trusts in you." - Isaiah 26:3 "Peace I leave with you; my peace I give you. I do not give to you as the world gives." - John 14:27
- "The Lord is near. Do not be anxious for anything, but in everything, by prayer and petition, with thanks-giving, present your requests to God. And the peace of God, which transcends all understanding, will guard your hearts and minds in Christ Jesus." - Philippians 4:5 -7

Rest:
- "Come to me, all who are weary and burdened, and I will give you rest." - Matthew 11:28

Healing, Health, Wholeness:
- "that you may be **filled** with the **fullness of God**" - Ephesians 3:19)
- "He has sen t me to preach good news to the poor, to bind up the broken hearted , to proclaim freed om for the captives, and release from darkness for the prisoners, ... to comfort all who mourn ... to bestow o n them a crown of beauty, gladness instead of mourning, and a garment of praise instead of a spirit of despair." - Isaiah 6 1:1-3
- " Bring my soul out of prison, that I may praise your name." - Psalm 142 :7
- Names of God:
  - "Jehova Rophe" - our healer, our health, and our wholeness
  - Jesus – "The Great Physician"

Others:
- **Salvation** (John 3:16, Acts 4:12, John 1:12; 14:6)
- **Forgiveness** (I Joh n 1:9)
- **Strength** (2 Cor. 12 :7-10 , Philippians 4:13)
- **Contentment** (Phil. 4:11 -13)
- **Power** (John 15:5, 2 T im. 1:7)
- **Comfort** (2 Cor. 1:3 -4)
- **Help** (I Peter 5:7, Hebrews 13:5-6)

GOD'S PROMISES

God's promises are ours (believers) to claim because of Jesus (2 Corinthians 1:20). Jesus paid for God's promises for us on the cross, and God fully intends to do and give what He promises.

- GOD DOES WHAT HE SAYS HE WILL DO (HE KEEPS HIS PROMISES)
- "WHAT I HAVE SAID, THAT WILL I BRING ABOUT; WHAT I HAVE PLANNED, THAT WILL I DO." - Isaiah 46:11
- "GOD IS NOT A MAN, THAT HE SHOULD LIE; NEITHER THE SON OF MAN, THAT HE SHOULD REPENT; HATH HE SAID, AND SHALL HE NOT DO IT ? OR HATH HE SPOKEN, AND SHALL HE NOT MAKE IT GOOD ?
  - Numbers 23:19

Because of God's **perfect faithfulness**, His Promises are really Guarantees. Here are some of God's promises, or guarantees, for His children... people who have a restored relationship with Him through His son Jesus Christ:

1. NEEDS

- "BUT SEEK *FIRST* HIS KINGDOM AND HIS RIGHTEOUSNESS, AND ALL THESE THINGS WILL BE GIVEN TO YOU AS WELL."   - MATTHEW 6:33

- " AND MY GOD WILL MEET ALL YOUR NEEDS ACCORDING TO HIS GLORIOUS RICHES IN CHRIST JESUS."   - PHILIPPIANS 4:19

- " I WILL SATISFY YOUR NEEDS..."   - ISAIAH 58:11

- " THE LORD IS MY SHEPHERD, I SHALL NOT WANT." - PSALM 23:1

2. WHEN YOU HAVE TROUBLES

- " CAST ALL YOUR ANXIETY ON HIM BECAUSE HE CARES FOR YOU."
  - I PETER 5:7

- "AND CALL UPON ME IN THE DAY OF TROUBLE; I WILL DELIVER YOU, AND YOU WILL HONOR ME." - PSALM 50:15

- " I WILL NOT LEAVE YOU COMFORTLESS: I WILL COME TO YOU."
  - JOHN 14:18

- " CAST YOUR BURDEN ON THE LORD, AND HE WILL SUSTAIN YOU."
  - PSALM 55:22

3. WHEN YOU ARE ANXIOUS

- "DO NOT BE ANXIOUS ABOUT ANYTHING, BUT IN EVERYTHING BY PRAYER & PETITION, WITH THANKSGIVING, PRESENT YOUR REQUESTS TO GOD. AND THE PEACE OF GOD, WHICH TRANSCENDS ALL UNDERSTANDING, WILL GUARD HEARTS AND MINDS IN CHRIST JESUS."
  - PHILIPPIANS 4:6,7

- "SO DO NOT WORRY. YOUR HEAVENLY FATHER KNOWS THAT YOU NEED THEM." - MATTHEW 6:32

- "LET THE PEACE OF GOD RULE IN YOUR HEARTS,... AND BE THANKFUL." - COLOSSIANS 3:15

4. WHEN YOU ARE AFRAID

- "SO DO NOT FEAR, FOR I AM WITH YOU; DO NOT BE DISMAYED, FOR I AM YOUR GOD. I WILL STRENGTHEN YOU AND HELP YOU; I WILL UPHOLD YOU WITH MY RIGHTEOUS RIGHT HAND." - ISAIAH 41:10

- " I WILL NOT FORGET YOU. SEE, I HAVE ENGRAVED YOU ON THE PALMS OF MY HANDS."   - ISAIAH 49:16

- also read DEUTERONOMY 31:8 ; PROVERBS 18:10 ; PSALM 34:4

5. WHEN YOU NEED ANSWERS / GUIDANCE

- "CALL TO ME AND I WILL ANSWER YOU AND TELL YOU GREAT AND UNSEARCHABLE THINGS YOU DO NOT KNOW."   - JEREMIAH 33:3

- " HE WILL CALL UPON ME, AND I WILL ANSWER HIM."   - PSALM 91:15

- "HE (THE HOLY SPIRIT) WILL GUIDE YOU INTO ALL TRUTH." - JOHN 16:13

- "FOR THIS GOD IS OUR GOD FOR EVER & EVER; HE WILL BE OUR GUIDE EVEN TO THE END."   - PSALM 48:14

- "I WILL INSTRUCT YOU AND TEACH YOU IN THE WAY YOU SHOULD GO; I WILL COUNSEL YOU AND WATCH OVER YOU."   - PSALM 32:8

6. WHEN YOU NEED WISDOM

- " IF ANY OF YOU LACK WISDOM, LET HIM ASK OF GOD." - JAMES 1:5

- "HE WILL TEACH US HIS WAYS, SO THAT WE MAY WALK IN HIS PATHS."
  - ISAIAH 2:3

- "TO THE MAN WHO PLEASES HIM, GOD GIVES WISDOM, KNOWLEDGE, AND HAPPINESS..."   - ECCLESIASTES 2:26

7. WHEN YOU NEED SECURITY

- PSALM 91

- PSALM 32:7 "You are my hiding place; you will protect me from trouble and surround me with songs of deliverance."

- PSALM 23

- PROVERBS 10:9 "Whoever walks in integrity walks securely, but whoever takes crooked paths will be found out."

- " GOD IS OUR REFUGE AND STRENGTH, AN EVER-PRESENT HELP IN TROUBLE." - PSALM 46:1

- " THE ANGEL OF THE LORD ENCAMPS AROUND THOSE WHO FEAR HIM, AND **HE DELIVERS THEM." - PSALM 34:7**

8. WHEN YOU ARE LONELY

- " AND SURELY I AM WITH YOU ALWAYS."   - MATTHEW 28:20

- " I WILL FEAR NO EVIL, FOR YOU ARE WITH ME."   - PSALM 23:4

- "I AM WITH YOU AND WILL WATCH OVER YOU WHEREVER YOU GO…"
  - GENESIS 28:15

- PSALM 139:7-12

9. WHEN YOU NEED COMFORT

- " PRAISE BE TO THE GOD AND FATHER OF OUR LORD JESUS CHRIST, THE FATHER OF COMPASSION AND THE GOD OF COMFORT, WHO COMFORTS US IN
  ALL OUR TROUBLES, SO THAT WE CAN COMFORT THOSE IN ANY TROUBLE WITH THE COMFORT WE OURSELVES HAVE RECEIVED FROM GOD." - 2 CORINTHIANS 1:3-4

10. WHEN YOU ARE DISCOURAGED OR FEELING DEFEATED

- " THE LORD HIMSELF GOES BEFORE YOU AND WILL BE WITH YOU; HE WILL NEVER LEAVE YOU OR FORSAKE YOU. DO NOT BE AFRAID; DO NOT BE DISCOURAGED."   - DEUTERONOMY 31:8

- " THANKS BE TO GOD, WHO ALWAYS LEADS US IN TRIUMPHANT PROCESSION (VICTORY) IN CHRIST"   - 2 CORINTHIANS 2:14

- "VICTORY RESTS WITH THE LORD." - PROVERBS 21:31

11. WHEN YOU NEED REST

- "FIND REST, O MY SOUL, IN GOD ALONE; MY HOPE COMES FROM HIM." - PSALM 62:5
- "COME TO ME, ALL WHO ARE WEARY & BURDENED, AND I WILL GIVE YOU REST." - MATTHEW 11:28-30

Faith is vitally important for walking closely with God and pleasing Him. When we pray and ask God to help us or supply our needs, we need to have faith and believe that He wants to help us and that He will. We need to have "believing prayer":

- BELIEVING PRAYER IS THE TRANSFER OF A PROMISE OF GOD INTO YOUR PROBLEM OR NEED OR CIRCUMSTANCES.
- GO TO GOD'S WORD AND GOD WITH YOUR PROBLEM, NEED, OR TROUBLES.
- PERSONALIZE GOD'S WORD TO FIT YOUR SITUATION. (WITHOUT CHANGING THE MEANING OF THE VERSE(S).
- READ GOD'S WORD ALOUD AND PLACE YOUR NAME IN THE PROMISE(S) THAT FIT YOUR NEED OR SITUATION.
- ALL VERSES AND PROMISES IN THE BIBLE LEAD YOU TO GOD, AND TO A PERSOANL LOVE RELATIONSHIP WITH HIM.
- MORE THAN ANYTHING GOD DESIRES FIRST FOR YOU TO OHAVE A RESTORED PERSONAL RELATIONSHIP WITH HIM, AND THEN CLOSE INTIMATE FELLOWSHIP WITH HIM, ONENESS & UNITY WITH HIM, AND A PARTNERSHIP WITH GOD IN HIS KINGDOM WORK & MISSION.

GIVE THANKS TO GOD

Giving thanks to God is very important, especially when you are having difficult circumstances. Even though you do not feel like giving thanks when you are struggling, it is a very important part of our prayer time with God, and it can help to lift your spirits.

- " GIVE THANKS IN ALL CIRCUMSTANCES, FOR THIS IS GOD'S WILL FOR YOU IN CHRIST JESUS." - I Thessalonians 5:18

- "DO NOT BE ANXIOUS ABOUT ANYTHING, BUT IN EVERYTHING, BY PRAYER AND PETITION, WITH THANKSGIVING, PRESENT YOUR REQUESTS TO GOD. AND THE **PEACE OF GOD**, WHICH TRANSCENDS ALL UNDERSTANDING, WILL GUARD YOUR HEARTS AND MINDS IN CHRIST JESUS." - Philippians 4:6-7

- "LET US COME BEFORE HIM WITH THANKSGIVING AND EXTOL HIM WITH MUSIC AND SONG. FOR THE LORD IS A GREAT GOD, THE GREAT KING ABOVE ALL gODS." - Psalm 95:2,3

- also read Colossians 2:6-7 and I Chronicles 16:34

* THANKSGIVING IS A KEY PART OF PRAYER; PRAISE TO GOD CONSISTS OF 2 PARTS:
- 1. ADORATION FOR HIS NATURE AND FOR WHO HE IS
- 2. THANKSGIVING

* THANKSGIVING DOES SEVERAL THINGS
- GIVES ALL THE GLORY TO GOD, WHERE IT BELONGS.
- IT IS A VITAL PART OF "BELIEVING PRAYER", ESPECIALLY WHEN YOU GIVE THANKS FOR **UNANSWERED** PRAYERS IN FAITH.
- IT HELPS YOU "COUNT YOUR BLESSINGS".
- IT LIFTS YOUR SPIRITS.
- IT BRINGS YOU CLOSER TO GOD.
- IT HELPS YOU REMEMBER ALL THE GOOD THINGS GOD DOES FOR YOU.

* THANK GOD FOR:
- HIS CONSTANT PRESENCE (Hebrews 13:5-6)
- ANSWERED PRAYERS
- HIS GREAT LOVE FOR YOU, HIS SON, HIS SALVATION,...
- YOUR SPOUSE, YOUR CHILDREN, YOUR FAMILY,...
- EVERYTHING YOU HAVE (HEALTH, FOOD, SHELTER, CLOTHING, JOB,...)
- EVERYTHING YOU DON'T HAVE (GOD KNOWS WHAT IS BEST FOR YOU)
- YOUR FRIENDS, YOUR CHURCH, YOUR PASTORS, YOUR S.S. CLASS,...
- EVERY THING GOOD OR BAD IN YOUR LIFE.

TRY THANKING GOD IN THE BAD THINGS THAT HAPPEN IN YOUR LIFE- GOD'S PEACE REALLY WILL HELP YOU THROUGH THE TROUBLE.
(see Romans 5:3-5; James 1:2-4; Romans 8:28-**29**; Jeremiah 29:11)

WEEK 3 STUDY REVIEW (Pages 103-112)

- REVIEW I CHRONICLES 4:9-10, PSALM 18:23-27 & 34:8, AND ISAIAH 30:18, AND THEN CHOOSE THE STATEMENTS THAT ARE TRUE:

___ One of God's "glory" characteristics is that He is good, and He loves to show His goodness to His faithful servants (those that are walking closely with Him).
___ God wants you to decide what you think is good for you and then He will provide it.
___ God will bless all Christians, even if they are not really interested in getting closer to God
___ God wants to "enlarge your territory" for Him and use you in His kingdom work.
___ Unless God's "hand" is with us, we cannot accomplish the things He wants us to (John 15:5)
___ We need God to protect us from evil so that we will not fall into sin & fall away from God.

- DID JESUS REALLY MEAN IN MATTHEW 6:33 THAT IF WE SEEK FIRST A RIGHT RELATIONSHIP WITH HIM AND BUILDING HIS KINGDOM THAT HE WOULD TAKE CARE OF EVERYTHING ELSE (ALL OF OUR NEEDS) ? CAN IT BE THIS SIMPLE ?

  - READ & STUDY PSALM 37:3-6 ; VERSE 4 SAYS THAT IF WE "DELIGHT" IN GOD, HE WILL GIVE US THE DESIRES OF OUR HEART. CHOOSE WHICH ONE IS THE CORRECT INTERPRETATION: (Hebrew "delight" means to be SOFT & PLIABLE)

___ If you delight in God, then He will give you all of your desires and dreams and goals,...
___ If you trust in Him and live to have a right relationship with Him, and you are "soft & pliable" and **submit** yourself to Him, then He will be able to place His very best plans and desires for you on your heart and He will be with you to carry them out.

- REVIEW THE VERSES AT THE TOP OF PAGE 100: WHY DO YOU THINK GOD WANTS YOU TO SUBMIT/YIELD/SURRENDER YOUR HEART & LIFE TO HIM:

___ He realizes that if you yield to sin (greed, selfishness, pride...) you become enslaved by it and can ultimately be destroyed by it.
___ He is a controlling person who just wants to dominate you and run your life.
___ It is only as you learn to "let go" & submit to Him that He can lead you to His best for your life, cleanse you and transform you to become more and more like Jesus, and He can begin to **fill you** with His **life** & health & wholeness and His love, peace, joy, patience, kindness,...
___ **Close & right fellowship with God** is the key to spiritual & emotional health and wholeness.

- REVIEW PAGES 101-102 AND GOD'S PROMISES ON PAGES 103-106 ... IS THERE ANYTHING LISTED ON THESE PAGES THAT YOU NEED OR LACK IN YOUR LIFE ? GO TO JESUS - "THE SOURCE" AND ASK HIM TO SUPPLY THESE THINGS.

- REVIEW PAGE 107 - GIVING THANKS TO GOD. IT IS EXTREMELY IMPORTANT TO YOUR FELLOWSHIP WITH GOD TO MAINTAIN A THANKFUL AND APPRECIATIVE HEART ATTITUDE IN YOUR LIFE.

Get face to face with God and prayerfully review this week's material. Ask God to show you how you can be closer to Him and more one with Him

FAITH IS VITAL TO INTIMACY WITH GOD

Faith is absolutely vital to having intimacy with God. God's word tells us that we cannot please God without faith. Because God does not think or act like we do, and to us He works in "mysterious ways", we will not understand many things that He is doing... at the time. Faith is not about understanding everything God is doing, but it is trusting and following Him even though we do not understand what He is doing.

Faith is knowing that because of God's perfect character and perfect faithfulness, He will do or give what He said said or promised. The Bible calls a lack of faith having a hard, unbelieving heart, which is not pleasing to God.

Faith and trust is vital in any relationship, especially in our relationship and walk with God. You cannot have a good intimate relationship without faith and trust.

- "BUT WHEN HE ASKS, HE MUST BELIEVE & NOT DOUBT, BECAUSE HE WHO DOUBTS IS LIKE A WAVE OF THE SEA, BLOWN AND TOSSED BY THE WIND. THAT MAN SHOULD NOT THINK HE WILL RECEIVE ANYTHING FROM THE LORD." - James 1:6-7

- "Was not our father Abraham considered righteous for what he did when he offered his son Isaac on the altar? 22You see that his faith and his actions were working together, and his faith was made complete by what he did. 23And the scripture was fulfilled that says, "Abraham believed God, and it was credited to him as righteousness," and he was called God's friend. - James 2:21-23

- "But without faith it is impossible to please Him, for he who comes to God must believe that He is, and that He is a rewarder of those who diligently seek Him." - Hebrews 11:6

WHAT IS FAITH ?
- "Now faith is the **substance** of things hoped for, the **evidence** of things **not seen**." - Hebrews 11:1 (KJV)

- "Now faith is **confidence** in what we hope for and **assurance** about what we do **not see**." - Hebrews 11:1 (NIV)

- "Real faith is not hoping to get what you want, but accepting what God gives you" - Adrian Rogers

- "Faith is **knowing God**, and knowing that He is able to do what He says, and that He **will do it**." - Henry Blackaby

* What God says in His word is the **truth** - not what you see or what you feel. Faith is not based on circumstances, or what you see of what you feel. In fact, many times our feelings or what we think we see or understand are often misleading.

* Jesus in John 14:6 said "I am the way, the Truth, and the life." Truth is not a person or a concept... truth is a person – Jesus. Everything He says or promises is always Truth.

* THERE ARE 3 STAGES OF FAITH:

1. LITTLE FAITH -- "I BELIEVE GOD CAN DO IT, BUT I'M NOT SURE HE WILL"
2. STRONG FAITH -- "I BELIEVE GOD CAN DO IT, AND I BELIEVE THAT HE WILL"
3. PERFECT FAITH -- "IT IS ALREADY DONE" (SUPERNATURAL FAITH)

The Perfect Faith is not naturally in us. By nature we are doubters, or it is difficult for us to fully and totally believe. The Perfect "It is already done" Faith is placed into us by the Holy Spirit. It is a supernatural faith only the Holy Spirit can give us.

* WE HAVE NO FAITH OF OURSELVES -- IT IS ALL FROM GOD:

- "For it is by grace you have been saved, through faith-and this is not from yourselves, it is the gift of God." - Ephesians 2:8
- "The apostles said to the LORD, "Increase our faith!". - Luke 17:5
- "fixing our eyes on Jesus, the pioneer and perfecter of faith. For the joy set before him he endured the cross, scorning its shame, and sat down at the right hand of the throne of God." - Hebrews 12:2

* PAUL HAD SUPERNATURAL FAITH, LOVE/DEVOTION, AND PASSION FOR GOD

- "The grace of our LORD was poured out on me abundantly, along with the faith and love that are in Christ Jesus". - I Timothy 1:14

* IT IS THE OBJECT OF OUR FAITH (JESUS) THAT BRINGS POWER TO OUR PRAYERS & OUR LIFE, NOT HOW MUCH FAITH WE HAVE:

- "He replied, "If you have faith as small as a mustard seed, you can say to this mulberry tree, Be uprooted and planted in the sea, and it will obey you"- Luke 17:6
- "Have faith in God." - Mark 11:22
- Then Job replied to the LORD: "I know that you can do all things; no purpose of yours can be thwarted." - Job 42:1-2

* FATIH IS KNOWING THAT JESUS HAS POWER & AUTHORITY OVER EVERYTHING IN THE HEAVENS AND ON THE EARTH:

- "Then Jesus came to them and said, "All authority in heaven and on earth has been given to me." - Matthew 28:18

- "The earth is the LORD's, and everything in it, the world, and all who live in it." - Psalm 24:1

- "Yours, LORD, is the greatness and the power and the glory and the majesty and the splendor, for everything in heaven and earth is yours. Yours, LORD, is the kingdom; you are exalted as head over all. 12Wealth and honor come from you; you are the ruler of all things. In your hands are strength and power to exalt and give strength to all. 13Now, our God, we give you thanks, and praise your glorious name." - I Chronicles 29:11-13

- "When Jesus had entered Capernaum, a centurion came to him, asking for help. "LORD," he said, "my servant lies at home paralyzed, suffering terribly." Jesus said to him, "Shall I come and heal him?" The centurion replied, "LORD, I do not deserve to have you come under my roof. But just say the word, and my servant will be healed. For I myself am a man under authority, with soldiers under me. I tell this one, 'Go,' and he goes; and that one, 'Come,' and he comes. I say to my servant, 'Do this,' and he does it." When Jesus heard this, he was amazed and said to those following him, "Truly I tell you, I have not found anyone in Israel with such great faith." - Matthew 8:5-10

- "Then he got into the boat and his disciples followed him. 24Suddenly a furious storm came up on the lake, so that the waves swept over the boat. But Jesus was sleeping. 25The disciples went and woke him, saying, "LORD, save us! We're going to drown!" 26He replied, "You of little faith, why are you so afraid?" Then he got up and rebuked the winds and the waves, and it was completely calm. 27The men were amazed and asked, "What kind of man is this? Even the winds and the waves obey him!" - Matthew 8:23-27

- "In the synagogue there was a man possessed by a demon, an impure spirit. He cried out at the top of his voice, "Go away! What do you want with us, Jesus of Nazareth? Have you come to destroy us? I know who you are—the Holy One of God!" "Be quiet!" Jesus said sternly. "Come out of him!" Then the demon threw the man down before them all and came out without injuring him. All the people were amazed and said to each other, "What words these are! With authority and power he gives orders to impure spirits and they come out!" - Luke 4:33-36

* THERE ARE GREAT POSSIBILITIES IN "BELIEVING PRAYER":

1. "BELIEVING PRAYERS" CAN MOVE MOUNTAINS:

- "Truly I tell you, if anyone says to this mountain, 'Go, throw yourself into the sea,' and does not doubt in their heart but believes that what they say will happen, it will be done for them. Therefore I tell you, whatever you ask for in prayer, believe that you have received it, and it will be yours. " - Mark 11:23-24

The mountains in Mark 11:23-24 are the insurmountable, impossible things in our lives. They are the circumstances and and challenges that are too difficult for us to handle... our problems, our difficulties, our bad habits, our sin...

* FOCUS ON GOD, THE MOUNTAIN-MOVER, NOT ON THE MOUNTAINS.

* YOU HAVE TO DEMONSTRATE YOUR FAITH IN GOD:
- Let your attitude show that you believe in God
- Let your thoughts show that you believe in God
- Let your actions show that you believe in God
    - "And the scripture was fulfilled that says, "Abraham believed God, and it was credited to him as righteousness,"[a] and he was called God's friend. You see that a person is considered righteous by what they do and not by faith alone." - James 2:21-26)

2. ALL THINGS ARE POSSIBLE WHEN WE HAVE FAITH:

- "If you can'?" said Jesus. *"Everything is possible* for one who believes." Immediately the boy's father exclaimed, "I do believe; help me overcome my unbelief !." - Mark 9:23-24

- "I can do all this through him (Jesus) who gives me strength." - Philippians 4:13

- "If you believe, you will receive whatever you ask for in prayer." - Matthew 21:22 (this needs to be combined with I John 5:14-15 and means that "you will receive whatever you ask in prayer *according to God's will*".)

* YOU CANNOT PRAY & LIVE POWERFULLY BY FAITH UNLESS YOU KNOW GOD INTIMATELY & HAVE CLOSE FELLOWSHIP WITH HIM.

- You need to be tuned in to God and one with His will in order to pray and live powerfully

- YOU NEED TO BE RIGHT WITH GOD: "Therefore confess your sins to each other and pray for each other so that you may be healed. The prayer of a righteous person is powerful and effective." - James 5:16

- YOU NEED TO BE ONE WITH GOD: "My prayer is not for them alone. I pray also for those who will believe in me through their message, that all of them may be one, Father, just as you are in me and I am in you. May they also be in us so that the world may believe that you have sent me. I have given them the glory that you gave me, that they may be one as we are one- I in them and you in me-so that they may be brought to complete unity. Then the world will know that you sent me and have loved them even as you have loved me. - John 17:20-23

- "Don't you believe that I am in the Father, and that the Father is in me? The words I say to you I do not speak on my own authority. Rather, it is the Father, living in me, who is doing his work. Believe me when I say that I am in the Father and the Father is in me; or at least believe on the evidence of the works themselves. Very truly I tell you, whoever believes in me will do the works I have been doing, and they will do even greater things than these, because I am going to the Father. And I will do whatever you ask in my name, so that the Father may be glorified in the Son. You may ask me for anything in my name, and I will do it." - John 14:10-14

* PRAYING IN JESUS NAME MEANS PRAYING ACCORDING TO HIS WILL & HIS HEART & HIS DESIRES, AND FOR THINGS HE PAID FOR AT THE CROSS. ULTIMATELY WE NEED TO PRAY SO THAT GOD WILL BE GLORIFIED WHEN HE ANSWERS OUR PRAYERS.

* BECAUSE OF JESUS, AND WHEN WE PRAY IN JESUS' NAME AND ACCORDING TO GOD'S WILL, WE CAN HAVE GREAT CONFIDENCE THAT OUR PRAYERS WILL BE ANSWERED:

- "This is the confidence we have in approaching God: that if we ask anything according to his will, he hears us. And if we know that he hears us-whatever we ask-we know that we have what we asked of him."   - I John 5:14,15

- "In him (Jesus) and through faith in him we may approach God with freedom and confidence." - Ephesians 3:12

- "Therefore, since we have a great high priest who has ascended into heaven, Jesus the Son of God, let us hold firmly to the faith we profess. For we do not have a high priest who is unable to empathize with our weaknesses, but we have one who has been tempted in every way, just as we are—yet he did not sin. Let us then approach God's throne of grace with confidence, so that we may receive mercy and find grace to help us in our time of need."   - Hebrews 4:14-16

*BECAUSE OF GOD'S PERFECT FAITHFULNESS, HE WILL ALWAYS DO WHAT HE SAYS AND PROMISES. AND NOTHING CAN STOP GOD'S PLANS
- "What I have said, that I will bring about; what I have planned, that I will do."
  - Isaiah 46"11
- also see Psalm 33:10-11 ; Proverbs 21:30-31 ; Proverbs 19:21

* DO YOU LIVE BY SIGHT, BY SIGNS, BY SECURITY, BY FEELINGS ? OR DO YOU WALK WITH GOD BY FAITH THROUGH GOD'S GRACE ?
  - YOU NEED TO LIVE BY FAITH, NOT BY SIGHT - 2 Corinthians 5:7

"WHEN GOD'S PEOPLE PRAY: THERE IS HOPE REBORN, THERE IS SIN FORGIVEN, AND MIRACLES YOU CAN'T EXPLAIN AWAY."

HOW BIG IS YOUR GOD ?

Revelation 19:6 -- GOD IS OMNIPOTENT / ALL-POWERFUL

Matthew 8:5-10; 28:18 -- JESUS HAS POWER AND AUTHORITY OVER ALL THINGS

I John 4:4 -- GOD IS MORE POWERFUL THAN SATAN

Genesis 1,2 -- GOD CREATED ALL THINGS JUST BY SAYING "LET THERE BE"

Deuteronomy 31:8, Acts 2:23 -- GOD PLANS & KNOWS ALL THINGS AHEAD OF TIME

Job 42:1-2; Proverbs 21:30-31; Psalm 33:10,11 --GOD'S PLANS ALWAYS SUCCEED

Psalm 33:13,14; Proverbs15:3 -- GOD SEES AND KNOWS ALL (HE IS SOVEREIGN)

I Chronicles 29:11,12 -- GOD OWNS ALL IN HEAVEN AND ON EARTH

Isaiah 46:11 -- WHAT GOD SAYS & PLANS HE WILL DO

Luke 1:37 -- NOTHING IS IMPOSSIBLE FOR GOD

Jeremiah 32:17 -- THERE IS NOTHING TOO HARD FOR GOD

Job Chapters 38-41 ; 42:1-2 -- GOD CREATED AND CONTROLS ALL THINGS

Isaiah 40:12-31 -- GOD'S AWESOME SIZE, POWER, WISDOM, & STRENGTH

GOD'S MIRACLES:

- Genesis 21 (Abraham has a son at an old age)
- Exodus 14 (God parted the Red Sea)
- Daniel 3 (Daniel and his friends not harmed in the furnace)
- Daniel 6 (Daniel not harmed in Lions Den)
- Matthew 14 (Jesus fed 5000 men + women & children)
- Matthew 15 (Jesus fed 4000 men + women & children)
- Luke 8 (Jesus calmed the storm)
- Luke 17 (Jesus healed lepers)
- The virgin birth of Jesus

WEEK 4 STUDY REVIEW (Pages 115-120)

- REVIEW PAGE 115; MARK A T FOR TRUE OR AN F FOR FALSE:

___ Having trust and faith in God is absolutely vital to an intimate, right relationship with God.
___ It pleases God when you do not trust Him and demonstrate faith in Him in your life.
___ Trust is an essential requirement for any relationship, including yours with God.
___ God expects your trust and faith in Him to be not based on any facts or evidence (Heb. 11:1)
___ Your trust and faith in God grows as you see Him demonstrate His faithfulness and goodness in your life and in the lives of others.
___ You can build up or strengthen your own faith in God by your own will power & effort.
___ One of the best things you can do is ask God to help you to trust in Him more.
___ Expecting God to do what He says or promises is "perfect" faith (this comes from walking with God and getting to **know Him**)

- READ **I TIMOTHY 1:12-14** ; WHERE DID THE APOSTLE PAUL GET HIS STRONG "PERFECT" FAITH IN GOD AND HIS GREAT LOVE & PASSION FOR GOD ?:

___ He made his very best effort everyday to trust in God and to love Him.
___ He realized that He needed to fully submit himself and his life to Jesus and fully depend on Him, and thus he was filled with Jesus' grace (strength, power,...) and Jesus' faith and Jesus' love & passion for God (filled & controlled by God's Holy Spirit - see Ephesians 5:18).

- REVIEW PAGE 116; CHOOSE THE STATEMENTS THAT ARE TRUE:

___ According to Luke 17:6 & Mark 11:23,24 Jesus means that if you just have faith in God you can do anything you want to do, and you can ask for anything you want to and it will be yours.
___ You have to match up I John 5:14-15 and other verses/chapters in God's word with these verses to see that Jesus was talking about that if you walk with Him in a **right relationship** and trust Him, you will pray more like He did -- "Father not my will, but your will be done", and you will thus be able to see God work in and through you in powerful ways.
___ If you start your day with fellowship time with God (worship, His word, prayer,...), and thus your focus and perspective is on God and on following Him, you will tend to be able to better demonstrate your faith in Him through your attitudes, thoughts, actions... throughout the day.

- REVIEW PAGE 118 & 119; MARK T FOR TRUE OR F FOR FALSE:

___ You cannot pray & live powerfully by faith unless you have **right fellowship with God**
___ Saying "I pray in Jesus name" is a magic phrase that unlocks all of God's power & blessings
___ Praying in Jesus name really means you want to pray in agreement with His will, or according to His nature or character, or for things that He paid for at the cross.

- REVIEW PAGE 120; DO YOU KNOW GOD IN THESE WAYS ? WOULD YOU LIKE TO ? ASK HIM TO HELP YOU WALK CLOSELY WITH HIM, AND TO REVEAL HIMSELF TO YOU IN REAL AND PERSONAL WAYS.

Get face to face with God and prayerfully review this week's material. Ask God to show you how you can be closer to Him and more one with Him

WAITING ON GOD & SUBMISSION IS VITAL FOR INTIMACY WITH GOD

Waiting on God is not easy for most people, especially when you are waiting for God to deliver you or help you in difficult circumstances. There are times in our life when God does not respond immediately to our prayers, or to our cries for help. It may seem that God is not aware of your difficulties or that He is not going to respond. These times can be confusing, and it may even seem like God is far away or just plain not listening.

Fortunately we have some insight and guidance in God's word to help us during the difficult times we have when we need to wait on God. There are some examples in the Bible of other people's struggles with God not responding immediately to their prayers, and having to wait on Him for deliverance or help. In this article we will look at some of these examples:

The story of Lazarus (John 11)

- "Now a certain man was sick, Lazarus of Bethany, the village of Mary and her sister Martha. It was the Mary who anointed the Lord with ointment, and wiped His feet with her hair, whose brother Lazarus was sick. So the sisters sent word to Him, saying, "Lord, behold, he whom You love is sick." But when Jesus heard this, He said, "This sickness is not to end in death, but for the glory of God, **so that the Son of God may be glorified by it**." Now Jesus loved Martha and her sister and Lazarus. So when He heard that he was sick, He then *stayed two days longer* in the place where He was." - John 11:1-6
- It says Jesus loved them, but he did not go immediately to help Lazarus
- In fact Jesus waited until Lazarus died, and then he went to them
- They must have thought "why would you wait, if you loved us ?". Imagine your thoughts and feelings if you were in that situation
- Your feelings & emotions and thoughts would not have been the truth about the situation, or about what Jesus was doing
- Here was Mary's reaction: "Therefore, when Mary came where Jesus was, she saw Him, and fell at His feet, saying to Him, "Lord, if You had been here, my brother would not have died." When Jesus therefore saw her weeping, and the Jews who came with her also weeping, He was deeply moved in spirit and was troubled. - John 11:32-33
- Jesus' reaction to Mary's words shows how much He cares for them (and for us)
- Jesus had something different in mind for this situation than Martha and Mary did. They thought he would come immediately and heal Lazarus
- Instead Jesus waited until Lazarus died, and then raised him from the dead
- The result was that God and Jesus were glorified, and ultimately many people believed that Jesus was the promised Messiah... "Therefore many of the Jews who came to Mary, and saw what He had done, believed in Him." - John 11:45

God is God, and we are not. God does not do things the way we would do them. He even tells us this in His word: "For My thoughts are not your thoughts, nor are your ways My ways," declares the Lord. For as the heavens are higher than the earth, so are My ways higher than your ways and My thoughts than your thoughts". - Isaiah 55:8-9

Even though waiting on God is difficult, we need to learn to trust God, especially in difficult circumstances when we do not understand at all what He is doing. Or when He appears to not care about us, or when it appears like He is not listening to our prayers or is going to answer. Going through these circumstances helps to strengthen our faith in the Lord.

Here are some other examples in the Bible of people who went through the experience of waiting on God. In some cases they needed to wait many years before God responded to their prayers or cries for help, or for something that God had promised.

- Job – Job suffered more than most people would ever have to suffer in their life. For a long time God never answered Job's prayers, and it left him feeling sorry for himself and very confused. Yet he never walked away from God.
- "Oh that I had one to hear me! Behold, here is my [w]signature; Let the Almighty answer me." - Job 31:35
- Finally God did answer Job: "Who is this that darkens counsel by words without knowledge? "Now gird up your loins like a man, and I will ask you, and you instruct Me! "Where were you when I laid the foundation of the earth? Tell Me, if you [a]have understanding, Who set its measurements? Since you know..." (Job 38:1 to Job 40:1 and Job 40:6 to Job 41:34)
- Job was humbled by the suffering and by God's rebuke. In the end Job knew God more intimately by experiencing Him, and said this: "I have heard of You by the hearing of the ear; But now my eye sees You; Therefore I retract, and I repent in dust and ashes." - Job 42:5-6
- In the end God restored everything Job lost two-fold, and Job has a deeper and more intimate knowledge and intimate fellowship with God. (Job 42:10-17)

- Joseph is another good example of someone going through years of difficult circumstances before God rescued him. Joseph went through 13 years of trials, suffering, and injustice. And that was after he was almost killed by his brothers and then sold into slavery by them.
- But Joseph stayed faithful to God, despite having to wait a long time for God to deliver him.
- God used the 13 years to mold and shape Joseph into the servant He could use greatly.
- Ultimately Joseph was released from prison and made 2nd in command of all of Egypt, and God used him to preserve the lives of Joseph's family and the lives of His people Israel.

- David went through 17 years of trials and fleeing for his life from Saul and his enemies. He had to wait 17 years from the time he was promised to be made king of Israel until the time he actually became the king.
- In Psalm 13 David expressed his struggle of having to wait on God for His deliverance and help: "How long, Lord? Will you forget me forever? How long will you hide your face from me? How long must I wrestle with my thoughts and day after day have sorrow in my heart? How long will my enemy triumph over me? Look on me and answer, Lord my God. Give light to my eyes, or I will sleep in death, and my enemy will say, "I have overcome him, and my foes will rejoice when I fall." - Psalm 13:1-4

- Abraham had to wait 25 years until God fulfilled His promise of a son. His son Isaac was born when Abraham was 100 years old.

- Moses had to wait 40 years in the wilderness until God called him to deliver His people from Egypt. Moses probably thought that he had blown it years earlier when he killed an Egyptian for beating one of his fellow Israelites, and perhaps he thought that he would spend the rest of his life in the wilderness.
- Imagine spending 40 years living in a wilderness after making a bad mistake. Most of us would think that God was done with us.

In 1995 I prayed that God would allow me to serve Him full time. I had a strong desire to join God in His kingdom work, and prayed that He would use my wife Nancy and I. And you know what happened ? Nothing.

I continued to run my business, serve in our church, and kept seeking Him and working on my fellowship with Him. Then 9 years later, early in 2004, God began to speak into my heart that some day I would sell my business and use our own resources to serve Him. It took another year and a half and a lot of prayer and time seeking God to discover what God's plan and vision was.

In June 2005 our oldest son John and I went on a mission trip with our church to Sao Paulo Brazil, and on that trip God spoke very clearly and strongly in my heart that we would serve Him as missionaries in Brazil. It took another 15 months to prepare for the move... sell the business, get our permanent residence visa for Brazil, sell our house... Our church in Marietta Georgia had a Brazilian church also, and God provided Portuguese classes for us for 9 months during this preparation time through a woman in the Brazilian church. God also gave me a very clear vision of what He wanted us to do in our mission ministry during this preparation time.

*WAITING IS ONE OF THE HARDEST THINGS GOD MAKES US DO, ESPECIALLY IN TROUBLES AND TRILAS, BUT IN END WE ARE FAR BETTER OFF FOR IT.

When we need to wait on God, it is one of the hardest things that He makes us do, especially during difficult times and trials. But in the end we will be far better off for the experience, if we can trust God and endure until He brings an end to the waiting time. When we look back at the difficult times that we have had to wait on God, we often see that these were very beneficial times in our lives spiritually. Our fellowship with God is often much deeper because of the difficulties and having to wait on God.

"Praise our God, all peoples, let the sound of his praise be heard; he has preserved our lives and kept our feet from slipping. For you, God, tested us; you refined us like silver. You brought us into prison and laid burdens on our backs. You let people ride over our heads; we went through fire and water, but you brought us to a place of *abundance*." - Psalm 66:8-12

"But now, this is what the LORD says- he who created you, Jacob, he who formed you, Israel: "Do not fear, for I have redeemed you; I have summoned you by name; you are mine. When you pass through the waters, I will be with you; and when you pass through the rivers, they will not sweep over you. When you walk through the fire, you will not be burned; the flames will not set you ablaze." - Isaiah 43:1-2

God's ultimate goal is for you to become more like Jesus... a person of honor, and high quality, Godly character, and a person of glory... "And we know that in all things (trials, difficulties, suffering) God works for the good of those who love him, who have been called according to his purpose. For those God foreknew he also predestined to be *conformed to the image of his Son*, that he might be the firstborn among many brothers and sisters." - Romans 8:28-29

* SOME ENCOURAGEMENT FROM GOD'S WORD FOR WAITING ON GOD:
  - "but those who hope in the LORD will renew their strength. They will soar on wings like eagles; they will run and not grow weary, they will walk and not be faint." - Isaiah 40:31
  - "Wait for the LORD; be strong and take heart and wait for the LORD." - Psalm 27:14
  - "Listen to my words, LORD, consider my lament. 2Hear my cry for help, my King and my God, for to you I pray. 3In the morning, LORD, you hear my voice; in the morning I lay my requests before you and wait expectantly." - Psalm 5:1-3

* REASONS WHY WE SHOULD WAIT ON GOD:
  - To receive God's direction and wisdom for our life. (Jeremiah 29:11-13)
  - To keep in step with God and His timing (Be One with Him)
  - God may need to prepare us first before He answers, and before He can use us in His kingdom work and mission
    - "He made my mouth like a sharpened sword, in the shadow of his hand he hid me; he made me into a polished arrow and concealed me in his quiver. " - Isaiah 49:2
  - To stretch and strengthen our faith (to teach us to trust Him fully)
  - God wants what is best for us
    - "This is what the LORD says- your Redeemer, the Holy One of Israel: "I am the LORD your God, who teaches you what is best for you, who directs you in the way you should go. If only you had paid attention to my commands, your peace would have been like a river, your well-being like the waves of the sea." - Isaiah 48:17-18
    - also see Isaiah 55:8-9
  - To ultimately experience God in new ways, and to grow in our experiential knowledge of Him and in our intimacy with God
  - To learn to be humble and to learn submission

* GOD'S PROCESS FOR MOLDING AND SHAPING US TO BE THE VERY BEST WE CAN BE (LIKE JESUS) SOMETIMES INVOLVES HIS DISCIPLINE – NOT PUNISHMENT, BUT MOLDING & SHAPING THROUGH TRIALS
  - "We wait in hope for the LORD; he is our help and our shield." - Psalm 33:20
  - "Yes, my soul, find rest in God; my hope comes from him." - Psalm 62:5
  - "Hope in the LORD and keep his way. He will exalt you to inherit the land; when the wicked are destroyed, you will see it." - Psalm 37:34

* OTHERS' STRUGGLES WHILE WAITING:
  - David - "My God, my God, why have You forsaken me? Far from my deliverance are the words of my groaning. O my God, I cry by day, but You do not answer; And by night, but [d]I have no rest." - Psalm 22

- Jeremiah - "I remember my affliction and my wandering, the bitterness and the gall. I well remember them, and my soul is downcast within me. Yet this I call to mind and therefore I have hope: Because of the LORD's great love we are not consumed, for his compassions never fail. They are new every morning; great is your faithfulness. I say to myself, The LORD is my portion; therefore I will wait for him. The LORD is good to those whose hope is in him, to the one who seeks him; it is good to wait quietly for the salvation of the LORD." - Lamentations 3:19-26
- also read Habakkuk 1

Although waiting in God is never easy, there are times in our lives when God will make us wait on Him. He wants and needs to teach us an important lesson that we all need to learn if we are to become mature, faithful, and fruitful disciples and followers of Jesus. The important lesson is to learn to wait on God.

We need to learn to not get ahead of God. We need to learn that His ways and His timing are always best. We need to learn that without Him we can do nothing (John 15:5) and we cannot produce spiritual eternal fruit on our own.

We need to learn that we have to be completely dependent on Him. We need to learn to be in step with God and His timing. We need to learn to be one with God, as Jesus and our Father are one (John 17).

We learn many important lessons when we learn to wait on God:

WHEN GOD IS READY, IN HIS TIME HE MOVES STRONGLY & SWIFTLY

- "I am the LORD; in it's time I will do this swiftly." - Isaiah 60:22
- God has a set time to do what He wants to do or what He promises to do
- When it is God's time, He will do what He has planned or promised quickly, strongly, and in a far better way than we could ever do it

A GREAT PROMISE & TRUTH FOR THOSE WHO TRUST IN & WAIT FOR GOD... GOD WILL ALWAYS ACT ON BEHALF OF THOSE WHO LOVE AND TRUST HIM, AND HE WILL GLORIFY HIS NAME IN THE PROCESS:

- "Since ancient times no one has heard, no ear has perceived, no eye has seen any God besides you, who acts on behalf of those who wait for him. - Isaiah 64:4

WE NEED TO LEARN TO WAIT PATIENTLY FOR GOD, ESPECIALLY WHEN ARE CONFUSED AND WE DO NOT UNDERSTAND WHAT HE IS DOING. GOD HAS A GREATER PURPOSE IN MIND THAN JUST FIXING THE TEMPORARY PROBLEM OR CIRCUMSTANCE

- "I waited patiently for the LORD; he turned to me and heard my cry. He lifted me out of the slimy pit, out of the mud and mire; he set my feet on a rock and gave me a firm place to stand. He put a new song in my mouth, a hymn of praise to our God. Many will see and fear the LORD and put their trust in him. Blessed is the one who trusts in the LORD, who does not look to the proud, to those who turn aside to false gods." - Psalm 40:1-4

* WE NEED TO LEARN TO WAIT ON GOD, AND LEARN THESE LESSONS:

- GOD IS NOT IN A HURRY !!! He wants it done right, not done quickly

- GOD HAS HIS TIME AND HIS WAY
    - Acts 1:7 - "He said to them: "It is not for you to know the times or dates the Father has set by his own authority."
    - 2 Peter 3:8 - "But do not forget this one thing, dear friends: With the LORD a day is like a thousand years, and a thousand years are like a day."
    - Psalm 75:2 - "I choose the appointed time; it is I who judge with equity."

- FAITH STRENGTHENS WITH USE

- INSTANT ANSWERS DO NOT MATURE US

- PATIENCE IS ONE OF OUR GREATEST NEEDS

- GOD WANTS TO MAKE US COMPLETE & WHOLE
    - James 1:2-4 - "Consider it pure joy, my brothers and sisters, whenever you face trials of many kinds, because you know that the testing of your faith produces perseverance. Let perseverance finish its work so that you may be mature and complete, not lacking anything."

- WAITING DURING TRIALS IS GOOD TRAINING:
    - see Hebrews 12
    - Malachi 3:3 - "He will sit as a refiner and purifier of silver; he will purify the Levites and refine them like gold and silver. Then the LORD will have men who will bring offerings in righteousness."

- WAITING BUILDS CHARACTER & BUILDS OUR HOPE
    - Romans 5:3 "Not only so, but we also glory in our sufferings, because we know that suffering produces perseverance; perseverance, character; and character, hope."
    - Isaiah 49:23 "Then you will know that I am the LORD; those who hope in me will not be disappointed."

- GOD WANTS TO TRANSFORM US TO BE LIKE JESUS
    - Romans 8:28-29 - "And we know that in all things God works for the good of those who love him, who have been called according to his purpose. For those God foreknew he also predestined to be conformed to the image of his Son."
    - 2 Corinthians 3:18 - "And we all, who with unveiled faces contemplate the LORD's glory, are being transformed into his image with ever-increasing glory, which comes from the LORD, who is the Spirit."

- WE NEED TO LEARN SUBMISSION
    - James 4:6-8 "But he gives us more grace. That is why Scripture says: "God opposes the proud but shows favor to the humble." Submit yourselves, then, to God. Resist the devil, and he will flee from you. Come near to God and he will come near to you. Wash your hands, you sinners, and purify your hearts, you double-minded."
    - James 4:10 "Humble yourselves before the LORD, and he will lift you up."
    - Isaiah 1:19-20 "If you are willing and obedient, you will eat the good things of the land; 20but if you resist and rebel, you will be devoured by the sword." For the mouth of the LORD has spoken."
- GOD WANTS US TO BE ONE WITH HIM AND INTIMATE WITH HIM
    - John 17:22-23 "The glory which You have given Me I have given to them, that they may be one, just as We are one; I in them and You in Me, that they may be perfected [g]in unity, so that the world may [h]know that You sent Me, and loved them, even as You have loved Me."

* See God's Spiritual Goals & God's Training – Page 130

Waiting on God does not mean sitting around and doing nothing until God is ready to move and respond. Waiting on God can be a very active time of spending extra time in prayer and in God's word, seeking Him and His voice. Because of this extra focused time alone with God, many people emerge from difficulties and times of waiting on God with a much deeper and more intimate fellowship with God.

WAITING ON GOD MEANS:
- TRUSTING IN HIM

- RESTING IN HIM
    - Matthew 11:28-30 "Come to me, all you who are weary and burdened, and I will give you rest. Take my yoke upon you and learn from me, for I am gentle and humble in heart, and you will find rest for your souls. For my yoke is easy and my burden is light."
    - "Take my yoke upon you"... Jesus is talking about submitting to Him, His will, His timing... and letting Him be in front and lead you. He is Lord, and we are His followers.

- HOPING IN HIM
    - Isaiah 49:23 - "Kings will be your foster fathers, and their queens your nursing mothers. They will bow down before you with their faces to the ground; they will lick the dust at your feet. Then you will know that I am the LORD; those who hope in me will not be disappointed."

- WAITING WITH HIM
    - Hebrews 13:5-6 - "God has said, "Never will I leave you; never will I forsake you." So we say with confidence, "The LORD is my helper; I will not be afraid."

* WAITING ON GOD MEANS:

- SEEKING HIM AND HIS WILL
  - "You will seek Me and find Me when you search for Me with all your heart." - Jeremiah 29:13

- GETTING RIGHT WITH HIM

- SUBMITTING TO HIM
  - Isaiah 66:2 - "Has not my hand made all these things, and so they came into being?" declares the LORD. "These are the ones I look on with favor: those who are humble and contrite in spirit, and who tremble at my word."

- IF THE REQUEST IS WRONG: GOD SAYS "NO"
- THE TIMING IS WRONG: GOD SAYS "SLOW"
- IF YOU ARE WRONG: GOD SAYS "GROW"
- BUT IF THE REQUEST IS RIGHT, THE TIMING IS RIGHT, AND YOU ARE RIGHT: GOD SAYS "GO".

GOD'S SPIRITUAL GOALS FOR YOU

1. INTIMATE FELLOWSHIP WITH HIM

- Jesus is your 1st Love, your 1st Priority, your Lord & Savior, and your best friend
- I Corinthians 1:9
- Matthew 6:33
- Proverbs 21:21
- John 15:4-15
- Revelation 2:1-4

2. COMPLETELY ONE WITH HIM

- You want and submit to God's will, His plans, His priorities, His purposes, His timing,...
- Luke 9:23
- Luke 22:42
- John 14:21-24
- John 17:9-11
- John 20-23
- Galatians 2:20

3. TRANSFORM YOU TO BE LIKE JESUS

- His character, His holiness and purity, His love & devotion for God, His love for people, His desire to seek & save the lost, His peace & joy & patience & kindness & goodness,...
- Matthew 28:18-20
- Romans 8:17-18
- Romans 28-29
- Romans 12:1-2
- 2 Corinthians 3:18
- Galatians 5:22-25

More than anything, God wants close fellowship with you, to have you join Him in His kingdom work, and He also wants to make you the very best you can be - like Jesus

TRAINING IN RIGHTEOUSNESS & INTIMACY WITH GOD
(The tools that God will use in your life to reach His desired goals for you)

1. GOD'S WORD (A LOVE LETTER FROM GOD)

- "All Scripture is God-breathed (inspired by God) and is useful for teaching, rebuking, correcting and training in righteousness (how to have an intimate right relationship with God and how to please God), so that the man of God may be thoroughly equipped for every good work (be fruitful for God and His kingdom). - 2 Timothy 3:16-17

2. GOD'S DISCIPLINE - PUNISHMENT

- " The people of Israel and Judah have provoked me by all the evil they have done - they, their kings and officials, their priests and prophets, the men of Judah and the people of Jerusalem. They **turned their backs to me** and not their faces; though I taught them again and again, they **would not listen** (to God's Word) **or respond to discipline**... (Israel was eventually conquered by the Babylonians as a result, but God eventually brought them back to Him) - Jeremiah 32:32-42

- "My son, do not make light of the Lord's discipline and do not lose heart when He rebukes you, because the Lord disciplines those He loves, and He punishes everyone He accepts as a son. Endure hardship as discipline: God is treating you as sons. ... God disciplines us for our good, that we may **share in His holiness**. No discipline seems pleasant at the time, but painful. Later on, however, it produces a **harvest of righteousness and peace** for those who have been trained by it. - Hebrews 12:5-11

- also see Deuteronomy 8:2-5 and John 15:1-2a

3. GOD'S DISCIPLINE - PURIFYING, MOLDING, RESHAPING, PRUNING

- Examples:
    - Joseph - 13 years of injustice, suffering... before he was lifted up
    - David - 17 years of trials, fleeing for his life... before he became king
    - Abraham - 25 years before his son Isaac was born
    - Moses - 40 years in the wilderness before God used him to set Israel free

- " Therefore, since Christ suffered in His body, arm yourselves also with the same attitude, because he who has suffered in his body is **done with sin**. As a result, he does not live the rest of his earthly life for evil human desires, **but rather for the will of God**." - I Peter 4:1-2

- also read Psalm 66:8-12, Malachi 3:2-3, James 1:1-4, John 15:1-2b

WEEK 5 STUDY REVIEW (Pages 124-133)

- WHAT ARE SOME OF THE THINGS YOU NEED TO WAIT ON GOD FOR ?:

___ Seek for, and then wait for God's guidance and leading before you make a decision.
___ You may need to wait for God to work through a problem or crisis, or even suffering. (as opposed to trying to work through it in your own way or time).
___ You may have to wait a long time in order to understand and see all that God was doing in a certain situation or circumstance in your life.
___ God may give you a promise and you need to wait on His timing for it to come about.
___ You may need to wait for God's provision for a need in your life.
___ You may want to be used powerfully by God in your life now, but you need to wait until He can work in your heart, to bring you closer to Him & more one with Him & His purposes.
___ Many times you need to wait on God for answers to prayer.

- REVIEW **ISAIAH 43:1-5**, **PSALM 66:8-12**, & **HEBREWS 12:7-11**; WHICH IS TRUE ?:

___ God would never allow trials and suffering in His children's lives because He is love.
___ The truth of God's word shows that He will use trials and suffering in His peoples' lives, and if they trust Him and submit to Him, He will bring them to a spiritual "place of abudance" (NIV) which is a far greater intimacy and oneness with Him, and more like Jesus).

- READ **PSALM 62:5** - WHICH IS THE CORRECT INTERPRETATION ?:

___ "Wait in silence" means to not talk to God at all during a trial or period of waiting.
___ "Wait in silence" means to be careful not to complain during your trial or waiting, as this greatly offends God.

- READ **ISAIAH 64:4** AND **PSALM 40:1-4** ; GOD PROMISES TO ACT ON BEHALF OF THOSE WHO WILL TRUST HIM, AND SUBMIT & WAIT FOR HIM !!!

- REVIEW PAGE 122; WHICH STATEMENTS ARE TRUE ?:

___ God is always in a hurry to get things done.
___ God is never in a hurry ; He is always more interested in getting things done right.
___ God is more interested in doing things in your timing.
___ God knows that by testing you, your faith will grow in Him as you see Him work.
___ God wants us to grow in faith and patience, to help us be more complete and whole.
___ Waiting on God is a very inactive time in your spiritual life.
___ Waiting on God is an extremely active time in your spiritual life, as God is purifying you and your character, and transforming you to be more like Jesus.
___ Waiting on God is very important in the process of learning to submit to God & follow Him.
___ You can be close to God and one with Him without learning to submit to Him.
___ Learning to get in sync with God's timing is critical in order to walk closely with Him.

- WAITING ON GOD IS: TRUSTING HIM, RESTING IN HIM, HOPING IN HIM, WAITING WITH HIM, SEEKING HIM, SUBMITTING & BEING RIGHT WITH HIM

- REVIEW PAGES 125-126; IF GOD ALLOWS TRIALS AND EVEN BROKENNESS INTO YOUR LIFE, HE WILL LOVINGLY WORK IT ALL OUT FOR YOUR BEST, ESPECIALLY WHAT IS BEST FOR YOUR HEART & CHARACTER, AND YOUR RELATIONSHIP WITH HIM.

Get face to face with God and prayerfully review this week's material. Ask God to show you how you can be closer to Him and more one with Him

PRACTICAL IDEAS FOR SPENDING TIME WITH GOD

1. FIND A QUIET "PRAYER ROOM" OR "PRAYER CLOSET" IN YOUR HOUSE. (MATTHEW 6:6)

2. A QUIET PLACE & CONCENTRATION & FOCUS ARE ESSENTIAL FOR INTIMATE COMMUNICATION WITH GOD.

3. IT'S BEST TO GET GOD EARLY IN THE MORNING: (PSALM 5:3 ; PSALM 90:14)
    - BEFORE YOUR DAY STARTS ; BEFORE YOUR MIND IS CLUTTERED WITH THE DAY'S TASKS & BURDENS.
    - BEFORE YOU DO ANYTHING, PRAY.
    - MANY TIMES JESUS PRAYED EARLY IN THE MORNING.

4. BE CONSISTENT IN YOUR PRAYER TIME (BUT DON'T GET IN A RUT):
    - SET UP A SPECIFIC TIME, A SPECIAL PLACE,...
    - GET INTO THE HABIT OF PRAYING EVERY DAY.

5. MAKE PRAYER TIME INTERESTING ; IT'S A CHALLENGE TO MAKE YOUR PRAYER TIME INTERESTING DAY IN & DAY OUT ; BRING VARIETY INTO YOUR PRAYER TIME.

6. ORGANIZE YOUR PRAYER TIME; BE PREPARED BEFORE YOU PRAY.

7. MAKE PRAYER BRIEF- YOU CAN PRAY FOR MORE PEOPLE & THINGS THEN. (Matthew 6:7,8)

8. PRAY FOR SPECIFIC THINGS & FOR PEOPLE BY NAME.

9. GOD HONORS PRAYERS FOR OTHERS.   (Job 42:10)

10. KEEP A PRAYER JOURNAL OR DIARY:
    - WE TEND TO FORGET WHO OR WHAT TO PRAY FOR.
    - WE TEND TO FORGET GOD'S ANSWERS & FAITHFULNESS.
    - WE TEND TO FORGET WHAT GOD TELLS US.
    - IT'S A GREAT BLESSING TO LOOK BACK AT ALL THE TIMES GOD HAS ANSWERED YOUR PRAYERS (IT STRENGTHENS YOUR FAITH).
    - YOU ARE MORE EFFICIENT IN YOUR PRAYERS.

11. PRACTICE GOD'S PRESENCE DURING YOUR PRAYER TIME & IN YOUR LIFE:
    - MAKE A MENTAL IMAGE OF HIM BEING ALONE WITH YOU.
    - PRAISE & THANKSGIVING ACKNOWLEDGES HIS PRESENCE.
    - VERBALLY TALK WITH HIM DURING YOUR PRAYER TIME & YOUR DAY
    - READ HIS WORD ALOUD DURING PRAYER TIME.
    - PERSONALIZE GOD'S WORD TO FIT YOUR CIRCUMSTANCES.

12. PUT YOUR FAITH IN GOD, NOT IN YOUR PRAYERS. (Mark 11:22)

13. PROUD PEOPLE NEVER PRAY POWERFULLY. (BE HUMBLE)
    - "HUMBLE YOURSELVES BEFORE THE LORD, AND HE WILL LIFT YOU UP"
                          - James 4:10

14. PRAY WITH OTHERS. (Matthew 18:19,20) (Acts 2:42)

15. PRAY WITH YOUR SPOUSE & FAMILY.
    - A FAMILY THAT PRAYS TOGETHER STAYS TOGETHER

16. WHENEVER YOU DO ANY SPIRITUAL WORK FOR THE LORD, GET SEVERAL PEOPLE TO COMMIT TO PRAY FOR YOU. (PREACH, TEACH, YOUTH WORK, MISSION TRIP, WITNESSING,...)

17. BE OPEN AND TRANSPARENT WITH GOD
    - See Psalm 62:8
    - See I Samuel 1 (Hannah's prayers to God)
    - See Habakkuk 1
    - See Psalm 13 and Psalm 22 (David)

THE KIND OF CHRISTIAN & CHURCH GOD WANTS
A SPIRIT-FILLED, FRUITFUL, VICTORIOUS CHURCH

What kind of Christian & Church does God want ? What kind of Christian and person does He want you to be (and all of His children to be) ? What does God want His church to be like ?

Many of us would answer these questions by using a combination of today's modern standards and our own personal opinions or wants (what we think the church ought to be or should be, or what we want the church to be).

To find out what God is looking for His children & followers and His church to be, we need to look into God's Word. The Bible is our authority and guide to find the kind of Christian & church that God wants and desires.

God has given us clear guidelines in His Word for the type of Christian and Church that God wants. He has also given us examples to follow... His Son Jesus, and the early church in the Book of Acts.

We will dig into God's Word the Bible and discover the 2 keys to being all that God wants us to be... The kind of Christian / disciple and church that God wants us to be, and that pleases Him. The kind of person and church that God can use greatly in His Kingdom work and mission.

We will start in John 15:8 - "This is to my Father's glory, that you bear much fruit, showing yourselves to be my disciples."

- God wants you and His church to be Spirit-filled, powerful, and fruitful
- God is greatly glorified by a fruitful Christian and church
- This verse is talking about the eternal, spiritual fruit that is produced when we are the kind of Christian and church that God wants us to be

Jesus' life here on earth, and the early church in the Book of Acts are our examples to follow in order to be what God wants us to be. In this part we will dig into Acts chapter 2 and discover the first of 2 keys that we need in order to be what God wants us to be.

* ACTS 2:42 - the First Key of Being a Spirit-filled and Fruitful Person & Church:

- Acts 2:42 - "They devoted themselves to 1) the apostles' teaching 2) and to fellowship, 3) to the breaking of bread and 4) to prayer."
- Question – if a church does all of these things: church services, worship, teach & preach the Bible (at least some parts of it), Bible studies, small groups, fellowships, prayer time... will it be a spirit filled & successful church ? (It appears so, but not necessarily)
- It appears at first glance that these things are the First Key thing we have to do in order to be the Christian and church that God wants - Bible study, eat together, fellowship, and prayer.
- All of these things are important parts of being a Christian and a church, but they are not the First Key - the vital thing you have to have in order to be what God wants you to be.
- We can do all of these things in a religious way, and our hearts can still be far from God.

- We can go to church services, hear God's word and study it, go to fellowships and small groups, and pray and be involved in the prayer ministry at church, and do them as religious things we are obligated to do. Or we can do them as part of a religious checklist that will show that we are being "good Christians".

- Almost all churches do these things in one form or another, but most churches today are not Spirit-filled, powerful, and fruitful churches. In fact many are dead or dying, especially in America these days.

- What matters most is where our heart is. We can do all of these things and still our heart can be far from God. We can be good religious and moral people, but our hearts can be far from God.

To find the First Key thing we have to have in order to be what God wants us to be - a Spirit-filled, powerful, and fruitful Christian and church, we need to look again and dig further into Acts 2:42:

- Acts 2:42 - "They **devoted** themselves to... here is the First Key:

The Greek word for devoted "proskartereo" is the strongest word in the Greek language for **COMMITMENT**. It literally means "to latch on and refuse to let go". The people in the early church in Acts were not devoted or committed to being good religious people, or to merely doing some religious things.

They were not devoted or committed to a church or to a denomination, or to an organization, or to a ministry. "To latch on to and refuse to let go" means that they "latched on to Jesus and refused to let go of Him.

- It means they were f*ully devoted and committed* to follow and obey ***Jesus*** - no matter where He leads, no matter what he tells you to do, no matter the cost.
- The early church in Acts lived in a very dangerous time for Christians. The same people that tortured and killed Jesus were still alive. This was shortly after Jesus died on the cross.
- They suffered a lot of persecution, and they could be arrested or even killed at any time for serving and following Jesus.

Despite the difficult circumstances and the high cost of following Jesus, they were totally devoted and committed to Jesus. Not just to doing some religious things... to Jesus.

- All of the apostles (the leaders & pastors of the early church), except John, died for following and serving Jesus.
- Stephen also died (see Acts 7), Paul and many others also suffered and died for Jesus.

Because of their total devotion and commitment to Jesus, they were the kind of people and church that God wants - and the result was a Spirit-filled, powerful, and fruitful church.

The Results and The Signs of Being a Spirit-filled & Fruitful Church (Acts 2:43-47a):
- Acts 2:43 - Everyone was *filled with awe* at the many wonders and signs performed by the apostles.
- a sign of God's presence & glory filling the church : awe, wonders & signs, miracles

- Acts 2:44 "All the believers were together and had everything in common."
- another sign of God's presence & glory : supernatural "agape" sacrificial love and "koinania" fellowship and unity.

- Acts 2:45 They sold property and possessions to give to anyone who had need.
- another sign of God's presence & glory : great generosity, unselfishness, love & concern for others (God's sacrificial "agape" love... the sacrificial love that Jesus displayed when He died on the cross for our sins).

- Acts 2:46 "Every day they continued to meet together in the temple courts. They broke bread in their homes and ate together with glad and sincere hearts,
- another sign of God's presence & glory : joy, gladness, contentment, sincerity (despite difficult circumstances, suffering, and the threat of dying for following Jesus)

- Acts 2:47a "praising God and enjoying the favor of all the people (good reputation)."
- another sign of God's presence & glory : sincere heart-felt true worship and awe of God.

We will look into God's Word to find the 2nd Key thing we absolutely have to have or do in order to be the kind of Christian & church God wants. If we have the 1st Key, if we are totally devoted and committed to Jesus and to doing whatever He commands us to do, then we will have the 2nd Key also. We will gladly do whatever He tells us to do and be whatever He tells us to be... no matter what the cost.

Now we will look at the 2nd half of Acts 2:47:

Acts 2:47b - "and *the Lord* added to their number *daily* those who were (joining the church ?) *being saved*.
- Question – how should we define success for a church ? Number of members ? Attendance ? How many programs we have ? How big the campus is ?

- We ought to define success as a Christian and as a church: 1) as doing whatever Jesus tells us to do, and 2) Is there eternal spiritual fruit being produced in our lives and in our service and in our church ?

- The eternal spiritual fruit shown in this verse is salvations. Many people were being reached for Jesus and saved... being forgiven of their sins and having peace with God, a new restored relationship with God, and eternal life in heaven.

Notice in Acts 2:47b that it is the Lord God that is adding to their number those who were being saved. It is God that produces eternal fruit, and it is God who receives the glory (see John 15:8).

- One of the Main Signs of a Spirit-filled and fruitful Christian and church is that there will be Eternal Spiritual Fruit (true success). Eternal Spiritual Fruit comes in 2 forms: 1) Salvations and 2) Spiritual growth of the believers (Lives are being transformed).

Notice also that Acts 2:47b says that "the Lord was adding to their number - *daily*" – this is significant, and it shows that His people, the church, was doing their part regularly in their *daily lives*. Following and obeying Jesus and doing their part that He commanded them to do was a *lifestyle*.

They didn't just do their part as a special event once in awhile, they regularly did their part in their *daily life*. Because they were fully devoted and committed to Jesus. And Jesus commanded them (and us) to "Follow me and I will make you fishes of men." Fishers of men are people who actively in their daily life tell as many people as possible about Jesus and how to be saved and have a restored relationship with God & eternal life in heaven.

The 2ND KEY to being the Christian & Church God Wants : faithfully joining Him in HIS mission.

- We MUST be *on mission with God* in order to experience God's presence /glory/ power in our church, and to see Him doing what only He can do.
- Our part is to join God in the work He is already doing and be on mission with Him... in our "Jerusalem" (local area), our "Judea & Samaria" (regional area), and "the ends of the earth" (as He leads). Acts 1:8

If participating in God's Kingdom work & mission, or being on mission with God is the 2nd Key in order to be the kind of Christian & church God wants, then it is *vitally important* that we understand what God's mission is. Many churches are dead or dying today because they are not filled with God's presence and glory and power. And they are not filled with God's presence & glory & power because their hearts are far from God, and they have abandoned God's mission for their own mission.

Question ? What is God's mission ? There are 2 Parts to God's Mission. We need to look into God's Word the Bible to find out what God's mission is. God clearly reveals in His Word what His mission and passion is, and that He wants His followers and the church to obey and faithfully participate in His mission:

- I Timothy 2:4 – God *wants (desires)* all men to be saved and to come to a knowledge of the truth.
- Missions is not about a mission trip, or a special missions or outreach event the church has a few times a year, or a special ministry for a small group of people with a special gift.
- Missions is all about God's heart, and His desire & passion for all to be saved... for all people to have a restored relationship with Him and eternal life with Him in heaven.
- God has such a strong desire and passion for all to be saved, that He sent His only Son Jesus to suffer and die on a cross... to make it possible for all of us to be saved. His love and desire & passion for this is very strong.

When Jesus was here on earth he stated the first part of God's mission very clearly:
- Luke 19:10 – "I came to *seek* and save the lost".
- He said he came to seek the lost because He knows people's hearts and He knows lost people very well. He knows that most lost people will not step foot into a church, so because He loves them so much Jesus went out to where they were, to share the Good News of salvation with them. His attitude was that He loved them so much, that if they were not going to come to Him then He was going to go out to them and try to help them to have a restored relationship with God.
- We need to follow Jesus' example, and love all people like He does and go out to them and try to help them to be forgiven for their sins and have a restored relationship with God... no matter what It costs.

Jesus knew that He was going to die on the cross and then go back up to heaven. Who was going to continue to go and do God's mission ? God had a plan:
- Matthew 4:19 – Jesus said "Follow me and I will make you fishers of men".
- Literally Jesus was talking to His disciples or His followers in this verse. These were the people who would become the apostles - the leaders and pastors of the new church in the book of Acts
- In most churches today, if anyone at all is doing God's mission of seeking and saving the lost, it is usually only a very small group of people. Maybe the pastor(s) and the leaders and a few others.
- Is this the way God wants it, only a few people participating with Him in His mission ?
- Before we look at that It is important to note that Jesus said "I will *make you* fishers of men". He doesn't say "go out and do your best at being fishers of men."
- He is saying that IF we obey Him and do our part and go out and seek and save the lost - share the Gospel with them - then HE will empower us to do the mission work. And He through the Holy Spirit will take care of the results too and produce the eternal fruit and success.

Jesus says this in a different way in Acts 1:8 - "But you will receive *power* when the *Holy Spirit* comes on you; and you will *be* my witnesses in Jerusalem, and in all Judea and Samaria, and to the ends of the earth. These are His last words to His followers before rising up to heaven, so they are very important words.

So, in Matthew 4:19 when Jesus says "Follow me and I will make you "fishers of men", is He talking only to pastors, full time missionaries, and church leaders ? Or is He talking to all of His people, every person in the church ? We need to look into God's Word to find the answer:
- Acts 8:1,4 – On that day a great persecution broke out against the church in Jerusalem, and *all except the apostles* were scattered throughout Judea and Samaria... verse 4 - "Those who had been scattered *preached the word wherever they went*."
- The apostles (pastors & leaders of the church) all stayed in Jerusalem, and all of the rest of the church, the regular people of the church were scattered to other places. Acts 8:4 tells us that all of the people who were scattered, the regular people of the church, preached the Word (the Gospel) wherever they went.

- ALL of the people in the early church understood that Jesus was talking to *everyone in the church* when He said "Follow me and I will make you fishers of men." And they ALL obeyed Him and did it, even though there was a lot of persecution and they could even die for obeying Jesus.

Here is the result of such total devotion & commitment to Jesus and obedience to His command in Matthew 4:19:

- Acts 11:19-21 - "Now those who had been scattered by the persecution that broke out when Stephen was killed traveled as far as Phoenicia, Cyprus and Antioch, spreading the word only among Jews. 20Some of them, however, men from Cyprus and Cyrene, went to Antioch and began to speak to Greeks also, telling them the good news about the LORD Jesus. 21The LORD's hand was with them, and a great number of people believed and turned to the LORD."

- The Lord's hand represents His presence, His glory, His resources, and His power... working through the regular people of the church and producing many salvations and eternal spiritual fruit.

- Because everyone in the church did their part, God was able to bless and empower them and He produced the results and the eternal spiritual fruit.
- They all saw God do great things because of their obedience and devotion to Jesus, and they were all in awe of God and the great things He did.

The 1st Part of God's Mission is for *all of us* to be "fishers of men" - to actively in our daily lives go and share the Gospel of Jesus Christ with as many people as we can.

There is a 2nd Part of God's Mission:

- Matthew 28:18-20 "Then Jesus came to them and said, "All authority in heaven and on earth has been given to me. Therefore go and *make disciples* of all nations, baptizing them in the name of the Father and of the Son and of the Holy Spirit, and teaching them to obey everything I have commanded you. And surely I am with you always, to the very end of the age."
- Once we reach people for Jesus and they are saved, they are new believers and babies in the faith. God wants us to help them to grow spiritually.
- God does not just want converts, He wants faithful and fruitful and Spirit-filled disciples (followers)
- All in the church are to participate in this part of God's mission, to make disciples.
- We are all to invest our time, efforts, resources,... into the lives of other believers, especially new believers, to help them to grow spiritually... to help them to grow closer to Jesus and more like Him.
- This is not just the job of the pastor(s) or Sunday School teachers, or small group leaders. It is the job of all of us in the church. We can all invest our time to help others to grow spiritually, to love them, encourage them, help them learn to read the Bible, help them to learn to pray and hear God's voice...

When we are faithful and do our part, then God will do His part and produce fruit - salvations and spiritual growth. And then we will be the kind of Christian & church God wants. A Spirit-filled, powerful, victorious, and fruitful Christian and church.

WEEK 6 STUDY REVIEW (Pages 137-144)

- REVIEW PAGES 137 AND 138. IS THERE ANYTHING IN THE PRACTICAL IDEAS FOR SPENDING TIME WITH GOD THAT WOULD IMPROVE YOUR RELATIONSHIP AND TIME WITH GOD ?
- REVIEW PAGE 132; WHEN THE WORD "DEVOTE" OR "DEVOTED" APPEARS IN THE BIBLE (Colossians 4:2, Acts 2:42, I Chronicles 22:19,...) WHICH OF THE FOLLOWING BEST DESCRIBES IT'S TRUE MEANING:

___ Commit yourself to trying your very best to pray, read the Bible, go to church,...
___ Make a commitment to being the very best Christian you can be.
___ Make a commitment to be a deacon or serve on a committee at church.
___ Completely surrender yourself and your life to Jesus, "latch on or take hold of Him" and follow Him **wherever** He may lead you (this is true love and devotion for Jesus).

- READ **ACTS 2:42-47** ; MARK THE STATEMENTS THAT DESCRIBE A CHURCH WHERE THE PEOPLE ARE FULLY IN LOVE WITH AND FULLY DEVOTED AND COMMITTED TO JESUS:

___ The people regularly spend time with God in prayer and in His word, and they are excited about Him and about being in His presence and about serving Him.
___ The people regularly pray together.
___ The people have a very special love and unity between themselves.
___ They see God's activity and see Him doing great and awesome works through them, and this increases their excitement and passion for Him even more.
___ The church leaders need to somehow whip up excitement & passion for God in the people.
___ The people are not caught up in the "cares of the world" or "idols", and thus are free to have an incredible relationship with God.
___ The people have a problem with giving their tithes and offerings for God's work.
___ The people have an indescribable joy and gladness in their hearts.
___ People who do not know Jesus as their Lord & Savior see the **activity** and the **presence** and the **love of God** in the people in the church, and they come to be saved.

- READ **Acts 2:47, Acts 8:1-4, Acts 11:19-21**; CHOOSE THE TRUE ITEMS: A PERSON FULLY DEVOTED/SURRENDERED TO JESUS IS:

___ A good church member who goes to church on Sundays and Wednesdays
___ A person who is fully committed to God's kingdom work and mission
___ A person who sets his/her own goals and desires and then prays for God to bless them
___ A person who is living to please Jesus by obeying His command to be a fisher of men
___ A person who is living for the "finer things" that life has to offer
___ A person who is not relying on themselves anymore, but is fully dependent on Jesus
___ A person who is trying to be in control of their own life
___ A person who denies self, seeks God's will, and then follows it - whatever it is.

- READ **REVELATION 2:1-4 & 3:14-19** ; IS THIS WHAT WE WANT GOD TO HAVE TO SAY TO US? I ENCOURAGE YOU TO <u>FULLY</u> SURRENDER TO JESUS & FOLLOW HIM, AND ASK HIM TO HELP YOU TO LOVE HIM AS YOUR **FIRST LOVE**.

Prayerfully review this week's material. Ask God to show you how you can be closer to Him and more one with Him

Made in the USA
Columbia, SC
24 April 2019